Plunking
Reggie Jackson

Plunking
Reggie Jackson

JAMES W. BENNETT

Simon & Schuster Books for Young Readers
NEW YORK LONDON TORONTO SYDNEY SINGAPORE

The author gratefully acknowledges the assistance of editors David Gale and John Rudolph. He is also indebted to baseball historian Dr. Donald Raycraft.

SIMON & SCHUSTER BOOKS FOR YOUNG READERS
An imprint of Simon & Schuster Children's Publishing Division
1230 Avenue of the Americas, New York, New York 10020
Copyright © 2001 by James W. Bennett
SIMON & SCHUSTER BOOKS FOR YOUNG READERS is a trademark of Simon & Schuster.
Book design by Paul Zakris
The text of this book is set in 10-point Sabon.
Printed in the United States of America
10 9 8 7 6 5 4 3 2 1
CIP data for this book is available from the Library of Congress.
ISBN 0-689-83137-4

FIRST
EDITION

Chapter One

That was the spring Coley Burke fell in love with Bree Madison. The timing was right because he was between girlfriends, but he had no way of knowing how mystifying the relationship would eventually become. Eventually he would discover that there was always more to Bree than met the eye. When there wasn't less, that is.

He saw her that day in the library, just before he got the blue slip that summoned him to the guidance office. Her hair was red, sort of. Not that grim, carrot-colored frizzy stuff though. It was more of an auburn, which reflected a coppery tint when she stood in the light. Right away, he liked it.

He'd seen her before, but this was the first time he'd ever paid much attention. One of the guys from the team, Kershaw, had been dating her a couple months ago, and still was, for all Coley knew. Coley was sitting at a table by himself, reading a *Sports Illustrated* article about a new spring training baseball park under construction in Jupiter, Florida.

Bree was rummaging in the reference book shelves just a few feet away.

When she asked him if she could set her things on his table, he said, "Sure." She plopped down her purse and notebook on the other side. The geometry text and the biology book confirmed what Coley thought: She was a sophomore. He was pretty sure she was new in school this year, but he had no idea where she might have transferred in from.

"Thanks a lot." She smiled at him before she turned back to the reference shelves.

"You're welcome." *Like the table belongs to me?* he thought. Her wraparound plaid skirt was short. It was secured by one of those oversize brass safety pins. Each time she stretched high to take down a book, he couldn't help staring at her shapely white thighs.

The blue slip, when it came, was delivered by Ruthie Roth, one of the office runners. Like Coley, she was a senior. The blue slip was a small form, about the size of an index card. It said he was expected to report to Mrs. Alvarez's office immediately. "What's up with this?" Coley asked.

"How would I know?" Ruthie answered smugly. "My job is to deliver, not interpret."

Ruthie Roth was large and loud. She wasn't exactly fat, but she was big boned and somewhat overweight. Her straight hair was cut shorter than usual, with a sort of grape-colored dye job.

"What happened to your hair?"

"I thought it would be silver gray, but it came out this purple color."

"Why the hell would you want gray hair?" Coley asked. As a member of the theater and art crowd, Ruthie already came in for plenty of teasing, mostly by the jocks; it didn't seem to make sense to ask for more.

"I need gray hair for the spring play. I thought I could grow my own. I guess I'll just have to wear a wig. That's why I cut it short."

"What's the play?"

"*Who's Afraid of Virginia Woolf?* I got the lead. Or one of the leads anyway."

"I never heard of it."

"Gee, that's a shock," said Ruthie scornfully. "I get to play Martha. I get to be overbearing and obnoxious."

JAMES W. BENNETT

Since he had known Ruthie for years, ever since grade school, Coley didn't engage in the teasing as a rule. But he couldn't resist saying, "Well, that ought to be easy enough."

"Funny. You mean I'm typecast."

"Let's just say you won't have to do much acting."

"Funny once, not funny twice. I didn't come here to schmooze with you anyway. There's the summons, you probably better get going."

"So what if I don't go to see Alvarez?" he asked her.

Ruthie shrugged. "You'll probably get suspended or tied to the whipping post or something, how do I know?"

"Let's say you looked for me but couldn't find me. Let's say you went to study hall but I wasn't there because I have this library pass. In other words, you couldn't find me."

"Let's say I've given you the note from the office, so I have to leave now." She turned abruptly and left, walking on bouncing steps toward the hallway.

Mrs. Alvarez was a counselor in the guidance office. She came right to the point, politely but firmly. "Mrs. Grissom has turned in a progress report on you."

"Oh, shit."

"Do I need to remind you where you are, Coley? This is the guidance office, not the locker room."

"Okay, I'm sorry. What's in the progress report?"

"As of last week you're not passing English."

"That's before she collected last week's journals," said Coley quickly. "The journal will pull me back up."

"Back up to what? A D?"

"Maybe a D, maybe a C," replied Coley, more aggressively than he intended. He didn't like the challenge in Mrs. Alvarez's tone of voice. He looked her in the eye across the desk. She was young, maybe in her late twenties, thirty at the most. She was attractive. A pink scrunchie secured her black ponytail.

"What's in your journal?" she asked him.

"I wrote up two book reports. One was on a book called *Hoops;* I can't remember the name of the other one."

Mrs. Alvarez persisted: "Your English grades were good up until your sophomore year. Your ACT scores aren't the best in the world, but you scored high on the verbal part. I can't think of any reason for you to be flunking English."

Why is she boring in on me like this? "Things happen," Coley said.

"What things?"

He wished he hadn't said it. "It's a long story. I'd have to go all the way back to ninth grade. It would be a bore for both of us."

"Do you think you know what bores me?"

"Never mind. I already told you I'm not flunking. Not after Grissom records the book reports in my journal."

"I think you mean *Mrs.* Grissom."

"Mrs. Grissom." *Alvarez is like barbed wire these days,* Coley thought. People said it was because of her husband's death; she just wasn't the same person.

"I assume you want to be eligible for baseball," said the counselor tersely. "When does practice start?"

"It already did. We've got three doubleheaders next week. The team gets to go to Florida over spring break."

"Florida? The baseball team gets to spend the first week of March in Florida?"

"Yeah." Coley couldn't help smiling, just thinking about the trip.

"Who's paying for this? Where does the money come from?"

"It's comin' from the Boosters. The Booster Club is takin' care of all the costs." He could have added that his own father was footing most of the bill himself, including the cost of the airline tickets for the entire team and the coaches as well.

Mrs. Alvarez was shaking her head. "If you aren't passing four subjects, you won't be eligible."

"I know the rules, Mrs. Alvarez." Coley looked at the poster taped to her desk that read, WHICH PART OF THE WORD NO DON'T YOU UNDERSTAND? The surface of her desk was clean and neat. There was a box of Kleenex with designer clouds and a Beanie Baby with green hair that served as a paperweight. In the corner was a five-by-seven framed photograph of her husband in military uniform. He'd been killed last fall in California in a helicopter accident while he was out on a routine surveillance. *That would be a freak for sure,* Coley reflected. *You'd have a better chance of getting run over in traffic. You'd have to be snakebit for that to happen.*

"If you cared half as much about academics as you do about sports, you'd get A's and B's in English. All your subjects." As she made this observation Mrs. Alvarez wasn't looking directly at him. She was more or less staring into space, like she was distracted.

He couldn't get pissed at her, not with that photo of her dead husband. He could only feel sorry for her loss. He waited a few moments before he said quietly, "I've heard it all before."

"I'll bet you never hear it about baseball, though, do you?"

Coley folded his arms across his chest and stretched his legs. "You'd lose your bet, Mrs. Alvarez. You haven't met my old man."

"If you're talking about your *father,* Coley, you're mistaken. I've not only met him, I've had a couple of conversations with him. If not for him, I don't think I ever would have gotten a handle on

ACT requirements and the sliding grade scale for college athletic scholarships."

Coley nodded his head before he said, "Yeah, he would know. He would know it all."

"I guess you're fortunate then. Your father takes an active interest in your future."

Coley sat up straight. "You could put it that way. Are we done now?"

"I guess so. I just hope you're right about the English grade."

"I'm good with that, believe me. I can't believe she turned in a progress report on me before she read those last journals."

"Like I said, we'll hope you're right."

Then he left. When he got back to the library table, he found that Bree was sitting in the chair across from his sports magazine. It was still open at the same page. She looked up from her encyclopedia and note cards. "I saved your seat," she declared with a smile.

Coley had to wonder why you'd save someone's seat in the school library; maybe she was making a joke. She had beautiful teeth when she smiled. Her complexion was clear, with high color in her cheeks. But her blue green eye shadow was overdone, especially at the corners, the way it often was by some of his mother's friends at the country club to hide an advancing case of crow's-feet.

Still smiling, she extended her hand across the table. "My name's Bree," she said. "Bree Madison."

He needed to rise out of his chair in order to reach across. He leaned his elbows on the table. Her hand was small and soft. When he took it, he felt awkward. "I'm Coley Burke."

"I know," she said.

The top button of her blouse was undone. He enjoyed the limited view of her breasts, which weren't huge but seemed substantial on her thin body. A faint pattern of freckles speckled the top of her sternum. "How do you know my name?" he asked.

"Oh, please. I may be a transfer student, but I'm not stupid."

He took the remark as a compliment, even though he was used to attention. Coley was one of the school's main studs, an all-around athlete whose baseball stardom had brought him an abundance of public recognition. He had been written up in the local and regional newspapers so often that his mother needed to keep buying additional pages for the scrapbook she kept. He had even been featured in a *Chicago Tribune* article. Coley had been interviewed so many times by television reporters that the procedure bored him.

But this moment seemed uncommonly inflating for some reason. He sat down in his chair again. *I may be a transfer student, but I'm not stupid.* Bree Madison was a definite turn-on. Especially right after having Mrs. Alvarez on his case and getting another lecture about being an academic underachiever.

In about two minutes the bell was going to ring. He closed his magazine. "How'd you like to go out with me?" he asked Bree.

"Go out? You mean a date?"

"Yeah, that would be what I mean. A date. How'd you like to go out?"

"Where would we go?" she asked.

Coley shrugged. "Wherever. Knight's Action, a movie somewhere, wherever you'd like."

"I thought Gloria Freeman was your girl."

"Why do you think that?"

"It's what everybody thinks," she replied. She was smiling, though, like she was teasing him.

"That's history," Coley said to her. "That's over."

"Does Gloria know it's over?"

"She knows."

"I bet she's not happy about that," said Bree.

He shrugged again before he said, "I guess she's not. Breaking up is hard to do."

"Very funny," said Bree. Students were on their feet by this time, anticipating the bell by collecting their books. Bree put her encyclopedia away before she returned to the table. "I'll go out with you," she told Coley, "but we're not gonna mess around."

The combination of these two declarations gave him second thoughts. "Who said anything about messing around? Did I say that?"

She was smiling again. "You didn't have to. Guys never have to."

"Oh, yeah? What're you, fifteen? Sixteen maybe? You're like the expert, is that it?"

Bree Madison giggled before she replied. "I wouldn't say I'm an expert, but I know what males usually want."

Her remarks were as surprising as her demeanor, especially, for some reason, her choice of the term *male*. While Coley was searching for words that would make a clever response, the bell rang.

Chapter Two

From the window in Patrick's shrine Coley could see the entire backyard. He could also hear the phone messages as they played back on the answering machine in his father's den, across the hall.

Their backyard was more than two hundred feet deep at the southeast corner, where it was also its widest. The irregular shape of their property, like that of their nearest neighbors, owed its shape to the winding contours of Laurel Creek, located beyond the redwood privacy fence.

His mother's passion for landscaping was evident. In the center of the yard there was a kidney-shaped plot of yew bushes surrounded by violets and a fieldstone terrace. The anomaly was the bull pen, near the back fence. His mother's name for it was "eyesore."

But it was a bull pen, just as surely as the one at Busch Stadium or Wrigley Field. It had an elevated dirt mound, with authentic pitching rubber, perched sixty feet six inches away from an official home plate, that old rubber pentagon with black margins. Ten feet behind the plate was a Cyclone fence backstop. A well-worn path connected the home-plate area to the pitching mound.

From this perspective, on the third floor of their trilevel house, Coley could even see the statue. It stood in the left-handed batter's box. Cast in bronze, it was a life-size replica of Reggie Jackson with the bat on his shoulder. It was blue green from years of weathering, and it had a speckled pattern of bird shit. Coley couldn't see these details from so far away, but he knew they were there.

His father had discovered the statue at some sports memorabilia extravaganza in Indianapolis in the mid-eighties, and then paid an ungodly sum of money to buy it and have it shipped. It was hauled to their house and installed in their backyard by the Ryser brothers, who bolted it into the ground on a concrete slab.

Coley couldn't remember a time when the statue wasn't a fixture in their backyard. He was only a toddler when it was brought to its permanent resting place. He had heard his mother complain about how "gauche" it was, especially on the day when it arrived, the day his father had pronounced it "unbelievable." "Yes, that's a good word too," his mother had replied.

The installation of the statue had prompted his mother to intensify her landscaping efforts on that side of the yard. The fruits of her labor were mature now, in a flared pattern of privet hedge and lilac bushes that concealed most of the bull pen from view, if you were standing on the ground.

But not from up here, not from Patrick's shrine. Not even the lilacs, by the time they achieved their full foliage in late spring, would completely screen the view of the statue from the vantage point of this upper floor.

Most of the messages on the answering machine were for his mother—people wanting to schedule appointments to look at houses on the market. While Coley listened with half his brain, waiting to see if there were any for him, he wandered with the other half along the framed pictures and trophies that adorned this room. He didn't come in here often.

Just about every award and honor ever bestowed upon his older brother, Patrick, was preserved on these walls and shelves. There was a Hall of Fame precision in their pattern of display, so as to highlight the huge color photo of Patrick in his Mets uniform. Coley called the room Patrick's shrine, although never out loud if his father was in earshot.

The robot's voice on the answering machine asked if he wanted the messages replayed. "No, thank you," Coley hollered across the hall. He'd turned the volume up so loud he couldn't even hear the rewind button kick in. He descended the short flight of stairs that led to the main level of the house.

If the upper level belonged to his father, the main level was all his mother's. The large living room, the nearly-as-large dining room, the kitchen, the laundry room, and the sun porch. Nobody else's. Nobody else's decision which pictures hung on which walls, which copies of *Good Housekeeping* rested on whatever coffee table, which flowers got planted in the flower boxes on the deck. No dirt, no dust, no clutter.

Coley took the steps rapidly down to the lower level, *his* level. The red shag carpet was old but still in good condition. The bigger area, which had once upon a time functioned as a family room, was twenty by thirty feet. A small couch and easy chair hovered near a modest TV-VCR entertainment center at one end, while a disorganized mound of sports equipment, consisting of bats, balls, shoes, gloves, football helmets, and assorted team jerseys, crowded the other. There were various team pictures on the walls, from high school as well as summer baseball leagues, in addition to huge posters of Ken Griffey Jr. and Michael Jordan.

On the ceiling directly above his weight bench was a nude photo of Cindy Crawford taken from a *Playboy* magazine. She was lying on her stomach, though, which meant the most crucial parts of her anatomy were hidden. Coley hated lifting, but if he had to do it, it eased the pain to have a view of the sublime.

His bed and study desk were in the bedroom, which was also spacious. When he got mail, his mother left it on the study desk.

Today there were three letters. Two were from college athletic departments—Indiana University and Murray State, specifically. Coley opened them and glanced at them ever so briefly before tossing them. He was still getting letters from colleges even though he had already signed a national letter of intent with Bradley. It was the reality of mailing lists that once your name was on them, they never seemed to take you off.

The third letter was from the Royals' complex in Fort Myers, Florida. It was signed by a player development representative named Bobby Esau. Esau's letter said he planned to be in Coley's region in about a month, looking at prospects. He hoped to see Coley pitch and wondered if they might be able to get together for a visit.

After he read through the letter a second time, Coley decided to keep it. This wasn't the first letter he'd received from a big-league organization, not by a long shot; but some of them were only form letters, not worth saving. He knew that *player development representative* was just a la-di-da name for *talent scout.*

Coley looked at the textbooks in the center of his study desk, stacked with the values survey he was supposed to do for human dynamics. They weren't in this prominent position by accident. His mother had placed them, just as purposefully as she had placed the mail. She had been urging him to take this homework along on the Florida trip so as to make some productive use of his free time. In his mind's eye he pictured Mrs. Alvarez seated behind her desk and staring at him with that arched eyebrow.

Right after that he thought of Bree, the girl in the library. He remembered her pale skin and her reddish hair.

He nuked two ham-and-cheese sandwiches in the microwave, then took them, along with a twenty-ounce Pepsi, out onto the deck to eat. The sun couldn't seem to drive the temperature above the 45-degree mark. He could only hope it would warm up by the time they got back from Tampa.

Illinois weather in early spring was often nasty for baseball, which was why Coley had wanted to sign a letter of intent with Southern Cal or Arizona or Florida. He hated to pitch in cold weather.

And those were only a few of the warm-climate schools that had offered him a scholarship. His father had nixed those options, even though they were prestige opportunities with the potential to maximize any baseball player's development and market value. Coley knew why—if he was that far away from home, his father's level of control would be reduced. If Dad was a father in the first place, he was an agent in the here and now.

He devoured his second sandwich nearly as rapidly as the first. Washing it down with the Pepsi, he walked clear back to the bull pen, where next to the mound there were two dozen baseballs in a plastic milk crate covered with a yellow poncho. Most of the balls were old, but some were in decent shape.

With no glove and the wrong shoes, he took one of the balls and stood on the mound in the stretch position. He wasn't sure if he intended to throw the ball or not. He stared at the rigid Reggie Jackson, dug in fearlessly, bat at the ready position. As he stood by himself in this spot it was only natural for Coley to think of Patrick.

Patrick was dead now, and had been for four years. The mementos in the shrine room would never—*could* never—change. But if that was the glory in it, it was also death; the things that could never change.

It was Patrick who'd shown him how to plunk Reggie Jackson so you could get a *gong* sound. Even then Patrick had a major-league arm, so it took more than simply hitting the statue in the right spot, you had to have some serious velocity as well. Coley remembered Patrick's demonstration clearly—how if you hit the statue just beneath its bronze rib cage, in precisely the right spot, there was a hollow resonance that produced a mellifluous *gonging* tone. It was sort of like tapping a wine glass with a spoon in just the right location.

It had taken Patrick six or eight pitches to plunk the statue just right. Other times, when he hit the shoulder or the kneecap or the elbow, there was a tinnier sound. Sort of a *clink* or *tank,* like a plucked guitar string when it isn't held down clean along the fret. It wasn't the same as the real thing.

"Won't Dad be pissed if he knows you're hitting the statue on purpose?" Coley remembered asking.

"Who gives a shit?" Patrick had replied.

Since Coley was only twelve at the time, he hadn't been strong enough to deliver the heat; not enough velocity. Even when he hit the statue squarely, he only got one of the *clinks* or a thin kind of *pink.* No *gong.* But Big Brother had encouraged him by saying, "Don't worry, your day will come."

Another memory associated with Patrick was as embarrassing and frustrating as it was vivid. He recalled the time Patrick was home for a weekend in June, between his tour of duty in the instructional league and the date he was to report to the Mets' complex in Tampa. Along with Mom and Dad, Patrick had come out to watch Coley's PONY League game at Washington Park.

Coley had been playing first base that day, which wasn't his usual position. He didn't like it. In the sixth inning a guy named Leon Tibbs came out of the baseline in a rundown play. His hard plastic cleats slammed into Coley's wrist and knocked the ball out of his glove. Tibbs was safe, while Coley had to scramble after the loose ball, which was rolling into foul territory. He got it in time to make sure Tibbs didn't advance, but then he sat square on his butt and began massaging his sore wrist. The ump called time.

Coley knew he had pain, but he also knew that the only real injury was to his pride. It was the humiliation of coughing up the ball in a tough-guy collision. He was content to sit there for a few moments and absorb any sympathy that the spectators might be inclined to spend on his condition. From the corner of his eye Coley was able to watch his family's reactions.

His mother made a steeple of her two index fingers while she chewed at her nails.

His father stood up abruptly to leave, by way of the exit behind the bleachers.

"Get up," he heard Patrick say. "For Christ's sake, get up."

After the game, by the time Coley got home, he had forgotten about the incident. The entire game, for that matter. He was sitting in the family room with an ice pack on his wrist, watching MTV and eating from a bag of Fritos.

That was when Patrick had entered the room and told him to get on his feet. Big Brother was wearing his Nike spikes and carrying his glove.

"What for?" asked Coley.

"We're gonna throw."

"We're gonna throw?"

"*I'm* gonna throw. You're gonna catch."

"My wrist hurts," protested Coley. "Besides, I'm tired."

"You ain't that tired and you can kiss off that little boo-boo on your wrist. Get up."

Patrick was tough. God, he was so *mentally tough*. Patrick had led him to the bull pen, where he stationed him behind home plate right after giving him the catcher's mitt. Standing on the pitcher's mound, Patrick warmed up only briefly before he started humming fastballs. Coley took them in the crouch, the motionless

Reggie Jackson looming above his right shoulder.

Patrick threw harder and harder. He kept them in the strike zone, but so far inside at times Coley was afraid the ball might nick the statue, which would make catching it like a foul tip. Patrick kept the ball in the 90 to 92 mph range. Coley was flinching each time, but he was making the catches just the same. He might have quit at any time, but it was the principle of the thing, to show his big brother what he was made of, never mind that Patrick's deliveries were power pitches even by big-league standards.

At the time, he was only thirteen years old, fourteen at the most. Humiliated but determined, Coley had tears running down his face. Fiercely, he tried throwing the ball back at Patrick each time as hard as he could, as if to do unto his big brother what was being done unto him, knowing all the while what a foolish attempt it was. By the time Patrick said they were done, Coley's hand was burning so hot he had forgotten all about the sore wrist.

The way Coley remembered that ordeal, his only consolation was that neither of his parents was there to watch it. Whatever agenda there was, it was exclusively between him and Patrick.

His mother's voice returned him to the present. She was standing on the deck, holding the cordless phone. She called to him, "The phone's for you."

Coley walked to the deck, where his mother was holding the phone. "Are you packed yet?" she asked him.

"Not yet."

"You need to get your things packed as soon as possible."

"Okay, okay." He took the phone and discovered it was his friend Rico.

"Bring that new bat you've got, that thirty-two."

"You want me to bring that bat to Florida?"

"Bring it," replied Rico. "I *love* that bat."

"A bat's a bat, Rico. Besides, I've got enough stuff to pack without draggin' a bat along."

"But I love that bat," his friend repeated. "You just bring it, and I'll take it off your hands. I'll take it on the plane, I'll take it to the hotel. It won't be no trouble for you at all, I'll take full responsibility."

"I'll bring it if I can find it," said Coley.

"You can find it."

Coley tried to remember where he'd put it. If it was in that disorderly pile of equipment downstairs, he might have to hunt forever. "I'll bring it if I can find it," he said again.

After he hung up the phone, he went directly downstairs, where he started some lifting. Flat on his back, he commenced a series of bench presses at 190 pounds.

He was on his twelfth rep when his father came down. He hadn't heard him enter the house.

When Coley's father saw him lifting, he said, "Good for you." Coley put the bar in the cradle for a brief rest but didn't release his grip on it.

"Are you ready for Florida?" his father asked.

"I'm ready."

"God, I wish I could go with you. I wish I didn't have these meetings."

Coley turned his head. His old man was removing his sport coat and loosening his tie. Ben Burke was a handsome man; everybody said so, and it was true. He was graying at the temples, but tall and lean. He even kept a year-round tan by regular visits to his health and fitness club. Coley tried to imagine how he might feel about him if he'd never met him before, if he were seeing him for the first time.

"Did you hear what I said?"

"I heard you," Coley answered. "You wish you could go on the trip with us. You'd like to be a chaperone and a coach."

"So? Whatta you think?"

"I think it'd be nice if you could go," Coley lied. In fact, it was a massive relief to him that Ben Burke wouldn't be anywhere near on this trip. The only time baseball was any fun was when he could play the game out from under his father's scrutiny.

"That's not what I meant. I meant, what do you think of your great good luck that you're on a high school baseball team that gets to spend spring vacation in Tampa?"

"I think it's great."

"Well, think about it. How many teams get an opportunity like you guys are getting?"

"Not many," Coley said. He turned his head back and stared up at the bar. He grabbed it again, wiggling his fingers to secure the right grip. His father was cuing him for another thank-you. He had put up most of the money for their airline tickets, but how many words of gratitude did he need? Hadn't Coach Mason already thanked him a thousand times?

"I got a letter from Bobby Esau," said Ben. "I thought you might want to see it."

"I got one too."

His dad shrugged. "Oh, well, take a look at this one anyway. Maybe it's the same, maybe it's different."

"Okay." Coley lifted the weights from their cradle and started a second series of slow bench presses. He inhaled and exhaled explosively each time he returned the bar to his chest.

"Now, when you're down in Florida," his father said, "I want you to concentrate hard on that front shoulder. Don't let it fly open, okay?"

This was his father's real reason for coming down in the first place. The pitching mechanics lecture. Coley had wondered how long it would take him to get around to it. Would it be the only lecture from his father's collection, or would he have to listen to the *I don't want to hear any report that you were batting right-handed* one? Or maybe the *I put up big bucks for this trip you guys are taking, I figure I've earned the right to lay down a few guidelines.*

"Okay," Coley finally said, without taking his eyes from the weight bar.

"We haven't made all these videotapes for nothing, and we haven't studied them for nothing."

"I know." Up, down, up, down, breathing in and out fiercely at the conclusion of each repetition.

"It's not the kind of flaw that you can correct overnight. And it sure as hell won't correct itself. You have to keep your concentration at all times."

Up, down. Up, down. Coley had heard it all a hundred times before. Or was it a thousand? But Coley was only listening with half his brain. He was staring straight up at the undressed form of Cindy Crawford and, in his imagination, trying to superimpose Bree Madison's face on it. He found it was easier thought than done. "Don't worry about it," he mumbled.

"I *do* worry about it, because it's important. Great pitchers aren't just made out of arm speed and physical talent. They combine that with the mental part—concentration and knowledge of pitching mechanics."

"Oh, yeah," Coley muttered. "That's what us great pitchers do." It was scarcely more than a whisper, because if his father heard him, there would probably be a big-time quarrel.

It was after eight in the evening by the time his mother returned from showing a house on the East Side. When she came down, Coley was in the process of packing his duffel bag, the big blue one with the silver Nike swoosh. She was still wearing the company blazer.

She'd made a stop at Von Maur's to buy him a handsome leather travel kit with rigid partitions that made places for toothpaste, deodorant, shaving lotion, and the like. She'd already put a new razor and a bottle of Tylenol in one of the small compartments.

"Thanks, Ma. It's real nice." He was in the process of trying to force the aluminum bat into the duffel bag, but it was too long.

"Why are you taking that bat?"

"Rico wants it. He asked me to bring it."

"Your team doesn't have bats now?"

"The team has lots of bats. He's just crazy about this one. Don't ask me why."

"I can't believe you're going to take that thing on the plane with you."

"I'm not going to carry it on," Coley explained, "it'll go in the cargo section with the rest of the equipment."

"It would seem to me that a bat is a bat," his mother declared.

"Yeah, me too. But it doesn't seem that way to Rico. Anyway, it's no skin off my ass; if he wants it so bad, I'll bring it along."

"Please watch your language, Coley. You're not in the locker room yet."

"Sorry." Weren't those the same exact words Mrs. Alvarez had used? "What did you want to tell me?"

"What makes you think I have something to tell you?"

"I can just tell, Ma. You think I don't know when you've got something on your mind?" He was trying to zip up his duffel bag. The bat was not going to fit inside.

"All right, I do have something." She sat on the edge of the bed, then straightened her skirt and the hem of her blazer before she said, "I want you to behave yourself."

"In Tampa, you mean."

"In Tampa, I mean. I want you to behave yourself and set a good example for the younger boys."

"I'll behave myself," Coley assured her. He looked down. He knew where she was going with this; he only hoped she wouldn't reach her destination. "I always behave myself," Coley said. And it was true. An academic underachiever he might be, but the closest thing he had to a reckless lifestyle habit was the occasional beer he drank on the deck of their house. No substance abuse or other manner of antisocial habits. Coley's idea of nightlife was staying up till 2 A.M. to watch basketball games telecast from the West Coast. In his room.

"You're the captain," his mother persisted. "You need to set an example."

Coley chuckled with a sliver of contempt. "I'll set an example, Ma. You have nothin' to worry about. But as for bein' captain of the team, nobody's impressed with that. No scout or recruiter in the country cares who's captain."

"*I'm* impressed. Is that okay? *I'm* impressed. You were elected captain by your teammates. It might not excite the New York Yankees, but it pleases me."

"Okay, okay. I told you not to worry."

She looked him straight in the eye. "I have the right to worry, Coley. The last time I sent a son to Florida to play baseball, he came home in a coffin."

There. She had to take it to the bottom line. She had to bring up Patrick's death, and she had to do it right before his bon voyage. Coley was almost annoyed with her; she could have stopped before taking it to the limit.

Almost annoyed. But he had seen her caught in the middle too many times. "This is different, Ma. This isn't the big leagues."

Her eyes were lowered now. He heard her say, "It might be different, but it's still baseball, and it's still Florida."

All he could think of was to repeat himself. "Yeah, but this is different." He resisted the urge to reach out and touch the back of her hand; physical modes of affection were not part of the family tradition.

His mother didn't cry. When she lifted her face to look again directly at him, her eyes were glistening, but no tears. "You say it's different and I hope you're right."

"This is a high school team with coaches and chaperones. It's not nearly the same thing as spring training camp for a major-league team."

"I hope you're right," she repeated. "But I've earned the right, Coley. I helped Patrick pack his things too."

When he finally answered, all he could do was repeat himself once more, as feeble as it might have been. "This is different, Ma," he said quietly.

Chapter Three

It wasn't a luxury hotel by a long shot, but they could still see the shining waters of the gulf from the small deck just outside their fourth-floor room. "Jesus Christ," exclaimed Jamie Quintero, a freshman pitcher, "that's the ocean, man. That's the *ocean*."

"It ain't the ocean," declared Rico Cates, a senior who was, along with Coley, the cocaptain of the team. "It's the Gulf of Mexico."

"Say what?" asked Jamie.

"You heard me. This ain't where you find the ocean. It's where you find the gulf."

"You're full of it," Jamie responded.

"If you don't believe me, ask Coley. And don't be such a hick, okay? You want to embarrass us down here, or what?"

When Jamie asked him if Rico was right, Coley couldn't help laughing. Rico's worldly posturing was comical, especially since he'd never traveled south of Evansville, Indiana. Of the three, Coley himself was the only one with any previous exposure to Florida. "In a way, Rico's right," he confirmed.

"In a way?" challenged Rico. "What does that mean?"

"In a way. You'd have to go to the east coast of Florida for the ocean. The Atlantic Ocean is off the east coast," Coley explained.

"That's what I said. We're on the wrong coast." Rico turned to Jamie for support. "Isn't that what I already said?"

"It's what you said, but you're still full of it. You have to be technical."

"How'm I bein' technical?"

"Well, it's just one big body of water, right? And Florida just sticks out in the middle of it. Am I right?"

"Goddamit, Quintero, havin' a freshman roommate is one thing, but there's no way we can get behind a hick. You understand?"

"You just have to be technical," Jamie repeated. Quintero was the only freshman on the trip, but he was a good player and a good kid. Coley liked him.

Let them argue about the ocean, Coley thought. By this time he was on the balcony, listening to their quarrel from a distance and with only a portion of his brain. He only knew how free he felt. He was going to pitch in paradise tomorrow, and his father was nowhere around.

He looked to the west, where the silvery water was visible in slivers between the hotels and parking lots in the late-afternoon sun. When Jamie and Rico came out to join him, he said, "If you want the whole truth, what we're lookin' at is Tampa Bay."

"Say what?" asked Rico.

"This is Tampa Bay. The Gulf of Mexico is farther out. I doubt if we can see it from here."

Rico attempted to save face by saying, "Okay, Tampa Bay, but it's like part of the gulf, okay? I mean, it's all part of the same thing."

"It's all part of the same thing," Coley said, still staring at the multitude of sailboats docked along a distant marina.

"So you ain't so smart after all, huh?" Jamie said to Rico.

"Piss off. It's all part of the same thing."

Before supper the coaches took the team—all eighteen members—for a stroll along the beach. Coley and Rico waded in the edge of the clear surf and tossed tiny shells across the surface of the active waves in a fruitless attempt to make them skip.

"I got a letter from the coach at Eastern," Rico was saying. It wasn't easy to understand him since his mouth was half full of a Snickers bar.

"What did you say?" Coley asked him.

"I said, I got a letter from the coach at Eastern."

"And?"

"He says they can't make any promises about a ride," Rico replied.

Coley shrugged. He dropped down to try and sidearm another of the tiny shells, the same way he might drop down to intimidate a left-handed batter. "It's early, bro; it's only the first of March."

"He also says they might offer me a *half* ride."

"That's not unusual for baseball scholarships. You know that."

"It doesn't do me any good to know it."

"Can you get that crap out of your mouth?" Coley asked him. "I can't understand what you're sayin'." He sidearmed another shell but watched it turn over like a feather in the stiff sea breeze.

Rico swallowed the last of his candy before he said, "It doesn't do me any good. Not a half scholarship. You know I can't afford it without a full ride."

"And I'm tellin' you, it's too early to worry. We've got the whole season for scouts and coaches to watch us play."

"Yeah. Easy for you to say. You can get any scholarship you want."

That was true. Coley was a coveted commodity among the network of college and professional scouts. But he said again, "There's still plenty of time, Rico. You never can tell what might come along. There'll be scouts from Eastern, Western, ISU, the U of I, all over the place."

Rico was stubborn, though. He said, "What everybody wants is power. Power pitchers, power hitters. That's what everybody is lookin' for."

"Not everybody." Since Rico was only five feet nine and 145 pounds, Coley could understand his apprehension. "If that's all people wanted, there wouldn't be any place in the big leagues for guys like Mickey Morandini or Joe McEwing."

"Yeah, yeah."

"I mean it. It's not just power that wins games. You just keep doin' the things you're good at—fielding, moving runners along, hitting the ball to all fields. Gettin' on base as often as you do. There's plenty of coaches smart enough to figure that out."

"If you say so." His friend was breaking open another candy bar.

"You can even get full rides in junior college now."

"You can?"

"You bet. And that can lead to Division One scholarships and even pro contracts. Chill out on this thing."

"You sure know a lot about this shit," said Rico, taking a bite.

"I ought to. I've lived with Patrick and my old man my whole life. It's just too bad there's no academic credit for it. I might actually get an A in something. Know what I'm sayin'?"

Coley could hear Coach Mason hollering at them from farther down the beach. It was time to leave. The coach was going to hold a team meeting back at the hotel immediately after supper.

Coley pitched the first game of their opening doubleheader at 1 P.M. the following afternoon. The careless liberation he felt on the mound, under the warm Tampa sun but out from under the vigilant scrutiny of his father, turned out to be a curse as well as a blessing.

Loose and free, and with a comforting sweat drenching his uniform shirt, he consistently overpowered the hitters from Tampa's

Hamilton High. He was not at all what the players from the host school had anticipated, although they had probably been warned to expect a pitcher with a major-league arm as well as a major-league future. What Florida schools expected from the occasional northern visitor was a team of wannabes on vacation, a sitting duck whose development lagged far behind their own.

But what Hamilton High got, in this first game at any rate, was Coley Burke. On his good days Coley could throw his fastball at 92 to 94 mph. On his better days he could throw it at that velocity and spot it in the strike zone. He could throw it up and in, just off the plate, or down and away, four to six inches out of the strike zone. Under these conditions there were very few high school batters who could deal with him.

On his best days he had all of the above, plus control of his slider, which he threw at about 86 mph. The slider, which had a nasty bite, usually snaked out of the strike zone at the knees.

This was one of his best days, even though the northern climate he had left behind had limited him to inside-the-gym throwing. Most of the Hamilton batters, when they swung at his slider at all, managed only a feeble wave of the bat, which amounted to little more than an indecisive lunge. An excuse-me effort. It was a devastating strikeout pitch, although when Coley had control of the fastball, he usually didn't need an additional strikeout pitch. And on this day he had full command of the number one.

Before the game Coach Mason had warned him not to push himself, since it was the first time he'd pitched under game conditions. So Coley was content to stay with the fastball, keeping it down in the strike zone, or if he threw it up, to keep it at least as high as the letters. It was a great sucker pitch, a fastball with some pop that was up high in the strike zone.

The only hit Hamilton High could manage came in the fourth

inning when their shortstop, a guy named Olivares, hit a chopper—a swinging bunt—that stayed fair down the third-base line, then beat it out. Then Coley forgot to pitch from the stretch; as soon as he started his windup, Olivares stole second base easily. When the next batter hit a chopper to third, Kershaw, who was playing deep, had to charge it; his low throw short-hopped the first baseman. Not only was the runner safe, but Olivares advanced to third. Coley watched from the mound as the first baseman, Ricky Huff, juggled the throw and had to come off the bag. Olivares rounded third and bluffed toward home plate, but Ricky walked straight at him, holding the ball, until he chased him back.

Coach Mason called time and approached the mound. The coach was an easygoing old guy, but he wouldn't tolerate a pattern of mental errors. He asked Coley if he was tired.

"Hell no, why would I be tired?" Coley asked.

"There's a runner on second and the third baseman throws to first. What do you do?"

"Oh, yeah. I forgot to back up third."

"You back up third," the coach confirmed. "You don't stand on the mound watching the game like a spectator."

"Yeah, I forgot."

"You also forgot you had a runner on first. You pitched from the windup. What's the matter with you?"

"Nothin's the matter," Coley answered quickly, although he knew immediately that the same free sense of disengagement, of being *out from under,* was undermining his concentration.

"If you think your stuff is so overpowering you don't need to pay attention to fundamentals, you'd better rethink."

"I don't think that," said Coley. "This is more or less like practice, Coach. When we have a real game back home, I'll have my head in it."

But Mason was shaking his head even before Coley finished the sentence. "Sorry, but that's not how it works. You ain't in the big leagues yet; this is not spring training, even if we *are* in Florida. But even if it *was,* you play the way you practice. If you don't concentrate now, you don't concentrate when you think it counts."

It wasn't the first time Coley had heard this axiom, not by a long shot. "Okay, okay," he said. "Jesus Christ, Coach, I might as well have the old man down here with me." It wasn't true, though. Ben Burke and Coach Mason might have been on the same page as far as the *letter* of the pitching law was concerned, but not the spirit. The old coach settled for firm and disciplined, while Coley's dad delivered reproaches with unequivocal passion.

"If you mean your dad, we could do worse," Mason declared. "Without his financial support we wouldn't even be here."

"I don't wanna hear it," Coley replied abruptly.

"Okay, then hear this: The score is only four to nothin'. It's only the fourth inning. The game's not over yet. Get your head in the game as well as your arm."

"Okay, okay."

Lee Edwards, a three-sport athlete with a Division I future in football, was the next batter. He had a big reputation, which Coley had read about in the morning sports page of the local paper.

Now that there were runners on first and third, Coley worked carefully from the stretch position. He still felt free and strong, even after Coach Mason's reprimand. He threw two strikes over the outside corner, one on the fastball and the second on the slider. Edwards was a good hitter, probably the best on Hamilton's team, but Coley had the count at 0-2.

Coley understood that good hitters, once they got behind in the count, weren't such good hitters anymore. Their confidence was down because they felt tentative. If they got into the guard-the-plate mode, they were more likely to swing at pitches out of the strike zone. Coley wasn't just a talent; he understood the craft of pitching. Years of clinics in the backyard bull pen with his father and his older brother, Patrick, had seen to that.

Coley threw Lee Edwards a too-high fastball, but Lee didn't swing at it. Then he saw Lee crowding the plate, something hitters liked to do when they could get away with it, to force outside pitches. The tape played in Coley's head: *You can't win if you don't pitch inside. The inside of the plate belongs to you, not the hitter. Hitters who are fearless are dangerous, while batters who have reason to be afraid are tentative.*

If there was one aspect of pitching that Coley had refined more than any other, it was how to knock batters off the plate. *You can't win if you don't pitch inside.* He threw Lee Edwards the fastball up and in. It was only eight or ten inches off the plate, but it was exactly where Coley meant it to be. Besides which, it had 93 mph of velocity and it had that tail. Edwards went down in a heap, his helmet flying off like a cork and the bat twirling to the ground near the on-deck circle.

When he got up to dust himself off and recover his equipment, he gave Coley a look. Coley just stared at him. They both understood the rules of engagement.

He struck Lee Edwards out with a change-up so devastating the bat flew out of the batter's hands. It landed next to the home-team dugout.

Chapter Four

That night after supper Coley used the phone card his mother had given him to call home. He made the call from the hotel lobby because the pizza party that was gaining momentum in their room was too noisy.

When his mother answered, she asked how their flight went and what the hotel was like.

"Everything's great, Ma. We've got the sun and the surf. Everything's great."

"You know I don't like it when you call me Ma. Did you forget anything? Is there anything you need?"

"Take a joke, okay? No, there's nothin' I need. Everything's cool down here. We're in the middle of a pizza party."

"Pizza parties are fine, but I expect you to help the coaches. Everyone needs to be accounted for. It's a big responsibility to take eighteen high school kids on a trip out of state."

"Everything's cool, Mom."

Then his dad picked up on the other phone. He told Coley it was warm enough to be sitting on the deck.

"It's warm enough here to be swimmin' in the ocean," Coley countered. "In fact, tomorrow we're gettin' some beach time before our first game."

His father was laughing. "I'm green with envy. Did you pitch today?"

"I pitched. We won the first game, lost the second."

"But you won the game you were pitching, right?"

"We won the game I pitched."

"So how'd it go? Give me some details."

"I was overpowering, Dad. I just blew them away."

"That sounds great, that sounds great." His father was chuckling. "Did you shut them out?"

"I shut 'em out. They got one hit."

"What was the hit?"

"It was real lame. It was just a little dribbler to third. Never got out of the infield." He was careful to make no mention of forgetting to back up third or being so absentminded he pitched from the windup with a runner on base. "Well, I'll let you go. I just wanted you to know everything is fine."

"Thank you for calling, Coley," said his mother. "I'm glad you're having such a good time—"

"Just a minute, hold on," his father interrupted. "Hold on, there. Can you give me a little more information about the game?"

"You mean the game we won or the game we lost?"

"Don't be a smart-ass, Son. You know what I mean."

Coley did know. The strategy of misunderstanding was his standard defense mechanism: play dumb. "I was awesome, Dad. Even these guys in Florida are overmatched."

"I told you not to be a smart-ass. Can you give me any more details about the game?"

"What else can I say? We won the game. I think it was four–zip. They only had that one cheap hit I already told you about. I think I struck out nine."

"You think?"

"Okay. I struck out nine."

"Did you walk anybody?"

"No."

"You didn't let your front shoulder fly open, did you?"

"No. Never, never, never." Coley turned his brain off until, some moments later, they hung up. He spotted Rico in the lobby store looking through the ball caps and Florida muscle shirts. He ended up buying chewing gum.

Coley joined him by the register, where he began leafing through a *Penthouse* while he waited for Rico to pay for the merchandise. "What happened, you get bored with the party?"

"Not exactly, but they ran out of pizza."

The picture of a very young naked girl on page 88 caused him to think of Bree Madison. He put the magazine away before they reentered the lobby.

"D'you know anything about Bree Madison?" Coley asked Rico.

"A little, not too much," his friend replied. He was opening a gum wrapper.

"So whatta you hear?"

"I hear she's hot."

"She is?"

"That's what I hear. Why?"

"No reason. I was just wonderin'." Coley knew this would be one of those elliptical conversations, because Rico would be breaking in two or three of the fresh sticks. But he asked anyway, "Who told you she was hot?"

"Kershaw told me."

"What does he know about her?"

"He was datin' her."

"Yeah, huh?"

Rico swallowed before he continued, "He was takin' her out for quite a while. He says she's hot."

"If she's so hot," Coley asked, "why'd he dump her?"

"That's not the way it happened. She dumped *him*."

"The little bitch." Coley chuckled. "She dumped Kershaw. How long ago?"

"Can't say for sure. Not too long ago, though, maybe a couple weeks."

"You know why she dumped him?"

"Nope," declared Rico. "I told you everything I know. Why do you care?"

"I'm not sure exactly. There's somethin' about her."

"What about Gloria?"

"Gloria's history; I told you that."

"That's not the way she tells it," Rico said.

Coley shook his head. "I think she's in denial."

"What's that supposed to mean?"

"You're in denial if you refuse to accept something that's actually true. People do it when someone close to them dies."

"Where the hell is this comin' from?"

"From Miss Wells. It's part of human dynamics."

"I can't believe you'd cut Gloria loose for good. She's such a babe."

"She gets to be real boring, bro," Coley informed him. "But if you're so impressed, you take her out."

"You think I could?"

"Not if you don't ask her."

It was after ten thirty curfew when somebody discovered Quintero was missing. "Where is he?" asked Nate Spears, one of the two assistant coaches. He was impatient. "I said, does anybody know where the hell Jamie is?"

Nobody seemed to know, or at least nobody was saying. The party was broken up and most of the team members had returned to their individual rooms, but Coley could see Kershaw and

Kuchenberg out on the balcony. It was hard to tell from this distance, but he was nearly certain he saw a smirk on Kershaw's face.

"Goddamit!" Coach Spears seemed inclined to swear at anyone in close proximity. "It's lights out in about an hour. If you know where he's at, I want to hear about it right now."

While Spears interrogated the few individuals still left in the room, Coley went out to the balcony. "Do you know where he's at?" he asked Kershaw.

"How the hell would I know?" was the response. Kershaw turned away, but not before Coley smelled the beer on his breath. Kuchenberg turned away too; he was giggling, but trying not to show it.

Coley pressed Kershaw again, "Just tell me where he's at if you know. I don't want him to get in trouble."

"Fuck you, Burke. I just told you I don't know."

Coley stood up straight. *So he does know.* Coley could feel his anger swelling inside. He and Kershaw had been antagonists for years, ever since junior high basketball. As much as he hated the thought of fighting, he didn't fear it. When he stood up straight, at six feet four inches and 220 pounds of well-defined muscle, the intimidation factor usually made it unnecessary.

"I don't want to hurt you, Kershaw," he said evenly. "Just tell me where he is."

Kershaw turned to face him. "What're you, playin' *captain?* Piss off."

"Just tell me."

"Who the hell do you think you are?" Kershaw spoke with his arms loose at his sides and his eyes staring straight into Coley's. Coley could feel the hair standing up along the back of his neck.

It was apparent that Kuchenberg, too, felt the tension generated by this unexpected face-off. "Hey," he said. "It's okay, just tell him."

"You can piss off too," was Kershaw's quick response. "I asked Burke who the hell he thinks he is."

"I think I'm the pitcher who would've had a no-hitter today," Coley replied quietly, "except our third baseman's such a jackoff he can't even field a little dribbler."

Kershaw's eyes were flashing. "Fuck you, Burke," he said again. Kershaw was a tough guy for his size, but there wasn't enough size for this occasion. He knew it and Coley knew it. His string of epithets was simply the proof.

Kershaw turned away to lean on the balcony again. He draped his arms loosely over the iron railing.

"Just tell him," said Kuchenberg again.

"I'll tell him shit," said Kershaw, still staring toward the gulf.

"If you don't tell me, you tell Coach," said Coley. "That means you probably sit out the rest of the trip. You'll get to watch us play though."

But it was Kuchenberg's discomfort that finally defused the potentially volatile situation. He said, "This is too much. This is goin' too far."

"So where is he?" Coley followed up.

"He's down on the beach," Kuchenberg replied with his eyes down. "Down by that tiki bar where we went wadin'. If you want me to go with you, I will."

"What's he doin' at the beach?"

"We pantsed him down there so he couldn't come back to the hotel."

"Jesus Christ."

"I'll go with you if you want."

"Kuchenberg, I oughta smack you one."

"Make sure you listen to the *captain*," Kershaw was saying. "Don't even think about crossin' the *captain*."

Coley was past the anger. Anything Kershaw might have to say could only be another feeble effort to save face.

Coach Spears went with him to the beach, but he was good and pissed. Coley was carrying a pair of sweats and his pitcher's warm-up jacket. "*Where* at the beach?" Spears was asking.

They were walking fast. "I don't know," Coley replied.

"It's a big beach. Where do you plan to look?"

"I don't know that, either."

"How did you find about about this? Who told you?"

"Look, Coach, I just found out, okay?"

"But who told you? Who left Quintero down here?"

"Can we just go find him and take him back to the hotel? Can you cut me some slack here?"

They found Jamie in waist-deep water, some sixty feet from the shore. Because he was naked, he was afraid to come out of the water. Coley could barely make him out because the lights from shore were faint at this distance.

"Jesus Christ," said the coach.

Coley was wearing his running shorts, but when he waded on out, the cold water rose above his waist. The chill night air had turned Jamie's lips blue and pebbled him with chicken skin. His teeth were chattering. He was hugging his own chest to try to stop the shivering.

Coley thrust the warm-up jacket at him. "Put this on."

"It'll get all wet," Jamie protested.

"Who cares? Just put it on."

Quintero slipped into the jacket, which was far too large but provided the advantage of covering his groin area when he moved to the shore. He squirmed into the fleece sweatpants, although they resisted stubbornly against the wet skin of his legs. The light was stronger here, while farther up the beach hotel guests were yukking it up at outdoor bars.

"Are you okay?" Coley asked him.

"I'm okay." Jamie shivered. Through his chattering teeth he added, "I'm gonna kill the motherfucker though."

Coley almost had to laugh, looking at Jamie's wiry but adolescent form nearly drowning in the huge clothes that engulfed him.

Coach Spears was close at hand. "Are you all right?"

"I'm okay, Coach."

"Are you warm enough?"

"I'm okay."

"Now, just who is it you're gonna kill? Tell me that."

"Never mind. I'll take care of it myself."

This time Coley *did* have to laugh. As small as he was, Quintero was spunky enough to take Kershaw on. He would get the crap beat out of him, but he would be willing anyway, just to get in a punch or two before he went down.

"Coley won't give him up either," said the coach.

Jamie was using the inside lining of Coley's jacket to wipe the water from his face and neck. "I said I'll take care of it, and I will," he repeated.

"What you'll take care of," countered the coach immediately, "is getting warm and dry."

"That'll be the first thing," Jamie murmured.

"And the second thing is you'll go to bed and get some sleep. And the third thing is you'll get yourself ready to pitch tomorrow. We want you to go at least five innings."

"You mean it?" Jamie was smiling.

"I mean it," confirmed Spears. "Would I lie about a thing like that?"

Coley was still smiling at him. He thought briefly about the earlier conversation he'd had with his parents. He was still pissed at Kershaw and Kuchenberg, and he felt sorry for Jamie, what they put him through. But it was so much better feeling like a man than like a child. "Since I didn't beat him up," he said to Jamie, "you have to give him a break too. You gotta pitch tomorrow."

As soon as he went to sleep that night, Coley dreamed of Bree Madison.

The following day they lost two games to Central High in Clearwater. The scores were 11-3 and 8-3. Coley played left field both games but didn't have to face any defensive challenges. The only balls hit his way were high, routine flies. At the plate he was always dangerous, of course, because of his athletic talent and his strength. But he never practiced hitting, because pitching was always the priority. He had one hit in the first game, a single, and walked twice. In the second game he got into a couple of the Central pitcher's lazy curves, but both times he got the ball slightly underneath. The results were majestic fly balls clear to the warning track, but they were both outs.

As promised, Jamie Quintero was the starting pitcher for the second game. He worked two good innings, but then he got wild and started walking people. A couple of errors and a long home run, and he was on the bench before he'd gotten anybody out in the fifth inning.

Coley watched the wiry freshman slump to the end of the bench, where he hung a wet towel over his head. Coach Mason let Kershaw pitch in relief. He wasn't too bad, but the score was 7-1 by the time the inning was over.

When they came in after the sixth, Coley went to the end of the bench to take a seat next to Quintero. "Don't feel too bad, Jamie."

"Easy for you to say." The muffled reply came from beneath the towel, but Coley could still discern the words.

"Yeah, I know. But don't feel too bad. You have to keep your head up."

Jamie removed the towel and sat up straight. He looked Coley in the eye. "Okay, my head's up."

"I mean mentally. I'm talkin' about your emotions. It's your first varsity game, and we're down here in Florida where these guys are way ahead of us."

"How many did I walk? Five? Six?"

"I wasn't countin'. The point is, you have to learn what you can do to get better."

"Now you sound like Coach."

Coley shrugged before he answered. "Well, maybe he's right."

"It's all easy for you to say, 'cause whenever you pitch, you just blow people away."

"Yeah, maybe, but not when I was your age. Not when I was a freshman. What you need to concentrate on is usin' your legs."

"Oh, yeah?"

"Yeah, you can't just pitch with your arm. Even when you drop down sidearm, you can't just throw with your arm. That's when you start walkin' people, because you get tired."

"Yeah, I know." Quintero lowered his head again while his elbows were planted on his knees. He held Coley in such high esteem he nearly deified him, so the advice wouldn't be wasted. Not in the long run. But Coley knew the little guy was too bummed at the moment to appreciate it. He dropped the subject.

They lost two games the next day as well, to another Clearwater team, Madison High. Coach Mason kept them after the second game to deliver a pep talk. He reminded them for the umpteenth time that the teams from the Sunshine State, having played competitive games for six weeks or so, were bound to be ahead of them in development. Therefore, their mission here was to work on fundamentals and developmental elements. Winning or losing would take care of itself. And later in the season there would be a payoff.

The guys were listening, more or less. But they didn't like losing five games in a row, never mind the particular conditions, and anyway, they were thinking ahead to beach time and another pizza party back at the hotel.

The next day they would be back in Tampa for another twin bill. On the way to the bus Coach Mason asked Coley if he wanted to pitch the first game or the second.

"I don't care. Why?"

"I got a call from a couple of White Sox scouts. They want to come out."

Coley shrugged. Pitching in front of major-league scouts was nothing new to him. "I don't care, Coach. Whatever you say."

"Okay, then, I want you to go in the first game again. Maybe we can get a mental edge, which'll help Kuchenberg in the second one. You think you're ready to go the distance?"

"You want me to pitch all seven innings?"

"If you think you're ready, I do."

"I'm ready. I'll be ready."

Coley pitched seven scoreless innings against Gulf Coast West. They won the game 3-0, to bring their record on the trip to 2-5. He felt strong and loose and grooved in the 88-degree sun. Gulf Coast had two hits, one a solid single through the hole, and the other a pop-up to short left, which Louie Stallings lost in the sun.

Coley struck out sixteen batters and walked two. In a word, he was overpowering. As soon as the game was over, the Gulf Coast coach came over to talk to him. "You're as good as advertised, kid. You're a helluva pitcher."

"Thanks." Coley was toweling the sweat from his face and neck, but hot had never felt better. Coley didn't know the man's name, but the Gulf Coast coach was a dumpy guy with a big wad of chewing tobacco in his cheek. He needed a shave. Brown dribbles ran down his chin among the gray stubble.

"You just blew us away. You picked a good day to do it too."

"What d'you mean?" Coley asked.

"Easterbrook and O'Connel were here from the White Sox. Sittin' right over there behind third base."

"Oh, yeah?" Coley didn't know the O'Connel name, but he remembered from lots of correspondence that Easterbrook was director of player personnel for the Chicago team. It would be something he could tell the old man when he got home, something that would occupy his mind. In the meantime, he needed to get away from this coach; the guy was gross.

They had to pack their things early the next morning. They were playing two games against another high school in Clearwater, but their flight home was early in the evening, which meant they would be squeezed for time.

Coley hit a home run in the first game, but they lost anyway, 10-2. The homer came in the fourth inning, and he got all of it. The ball elevated quickly, then sailed on out over the Cyclone fence and the row of palm trees, eventually landing in a 7-Eleven parking lot. It traveled at least 420 feet. One of the Clearwater coaches said it was the longest homer he'd ever witnessed on this field. Coley didn't get much of a rush from it; the team was still losing.

The Clearwater team pitched a left-hander in the second game, so he had to sit out. One of his father's rules, and one in which Coach Mason was thoroughly schooled, was that Coley was not allowed to bat right-handed under any circumstances. As a right-

JAMES W. BENNETT

handed batter he was nearly as good as he was from the left side, but it exposed his left arm.

Quintero got another chance on the mound. Because he had worked three strong innings, the game was tied 1-1 heading into the fourth. "He's gonna be a helluva pitcher one day," said Coach Spears.

Coley, who was squirming on the bench nearby, agreed. "Oh, yeah. For sure."

But the fourth inning was a rocky one for the freshman. A couple of walks, a wild pitch, an error, a solid double down the line, and they were behind 5-1. Quintero slammed his glove in the dugout after the third out. He commenced some angry pacing and a lot of cursing under his breath so Coach wouldn't hear. When he finally took his seat on the bench, it was next to Coley.

"When there's runners on and you come to the set position," Coley said, "you're pitchin' too quick."

"Oh, yeah?"

"Yeah. You're gonna get called for a balk. Hold the set position at least one more count. Say 'a thousand one' to yourself, then take a deep breath in and out."

"Okay."

"It'll freeze the runner all the way, and it'll put you in a comfort zone before you throw."

"Okay, Coley."

In the fifth, Kershaw doubled to left, and so did Kuchenberg. It was Kershaw's third hit and Kuchenberg's second. "We're startin' to hit," said Coach Mason. "We're startin' to get comfortable at the plate."

It was true, but Coley knew it was also a sales pitch. *Don't worry about winning and losing. We came to Florida because it's an opportunity to get better, and that's what's happening.* "We're still losin'," said Coley quietly, without looking in the coach's direction.

"All of this will pay off later in the spring."

"Right."

Lovell and Ingram were finding the groove as well. They both homered in the sixth, Lovell's coming with a man on. Suddenly the game was tied 6-6 with one inning to go. Spirits soared in the dugout, where Lovell and Ingram were getting pounded on the back. There was a lot of indiscriminate chest thumping, and Coley found himself on board all the way. The game was still tied in the top of the seventh when he talked Coach Mason into letting him bat. It wasn't easy. "This guy's a left-hander, Coley. If I let you bat right-handed, your dad would skin me alive."

"He doesn't have to know about it."

"Oh, please."

"We've got runners on second and third and only one out, Coach; all I have to do is hit a long fly."

"You think I'm blind here? Maybe you'd like to explain the infield-fly rule to me in words of two syllables or less."

"Sorry."

"If you bat right-handed, it exposes your pitching arm."

"But this guy's got nothin', Coach. Especially now that he's tired. I've gotta hit. *Please* let me hit."

"Let him hit, Coach," said Quintero. "All we need is one run."

"You stay out of this. This guy is wild, Coley. He's got five walks already, plus two wild pitches. If he tries to come inside, he could plunk you right on the elbow."

"This guy can't hit my arm or anything else. He's got nothin'."

"Let him hit, Coach." This time it was Rico speaking up; as a senior cocaptain he was a more persuasive lobbyist than any freshman. "The bottom line is, we can win the game."

Coach Mason was staring out at center field, clearly tempted, but just as clearly on the horns of a dilemma. The umpire was approaching the dugout, impatient for a decision. "Have you got a hitter, or what?" he asked.

The coach turned to Coley. He spoke quietly. "You'd have to wear Lovell's arm guard."

"I don't care," he lied. He hated the idea of wearing the arm guard, which was like a soft cast with a flexible hinge, covered by hard plastic. Because it was stiff and cumbersome, it would limit his range of motion when swinging the bat. But he knew better than to press his luck. "Whatever you say, Coach."

"Because I'm not letting you hit unless you wear it."

"You're the boss," said Coley with a smile.

"Am I really?" Mason didn't wait for an answer. He turned to the restless umpire to give him Coley's name as a pinch hitter.

Coley strapped on the arm guard as he approached the plate slowly. He took several ballistic swings with the heaviest bat in the collection to try to feel loose with a restricted left elbow.

"Okay, let's go." The ump was long out of patience.

"You the man, Coley!" he could hear Quintero shouting. "You the *man!*"

Coley just watched the first two pitches to see what the Clearwater lefty had. It wasn't much. The second pitch was a strike on a dinky curve about letter high.

Throw me that curve one more time, he thought to himself as he dug in for the next pitch. The next pitch was the same one, a hanging curve up in the strike zone. Coley mashed it, immensely high and far to straightaway center. He had gotten under it just a touch, so it wasn't going to clear the fence, but it would back the center fielder up as far as he could go.

Coley was jogging halfway between first and second when the

catch was made. He began unstrapping the arm guard while the center fielder was still waiting for the ball to come down. Kershaw, who was the runner at third, scored easily. It was Coley's turn to take a pounding between the shoulder blades from his teammates.

He was ready to pitch the bottom half of the inning if needed, but it wasn't necessary. His teammates held on for the win.

Chapter Five

Coley pitched the first home game of the season against Peoria Richwoods the following week. He didn't have his best stuff, but he was more than Richwoods could handle. He walked too many batters—six—but he also recorded eleven strikeouts. He only allowed two hits, both singles and both on the infield. They won the game, 9-1.

It was a blustery day with dirt blowing around and the temperature no higher than the middle fifties. Chilly conditions usually affected Coley's control. Today he was wild high, but not by much. His high hard one, particularly when it was out of the strike zone but not above the armpits, was an effective strikeout pitch. Between innings he bundled up with a towel around his neck, stuffed inside the collar of his letter jacket. He couldn't help thinking glumly of Tampa and Clearwater, and the warm sunshine.

The sixth inning typified his shaky dominance. After walking the first two batters, he gave up one of the two hits, a chopper to his left that Lovell, the second baseman, couldn't flag down in time. Then he threw a wild pitch in the dirt, which allowed a run to score. He struck out the next three batters to end the inning.

His father wasn't there for the whole game but had arrived in time to watch the last three innings. When the game was over, he approached Coley near the dugout. "When you're wild high like that, what does it mean?"

"It means I'm gonna walk too many people," Coley replied. "Except for the guys who can't lay off the high one."

"Now, don't be a smart-ass. You know what I'm asking. If you're wild high, what does that tell you?"

Coley's left arm and shoulder were wrapped in a big, fluffy towel. He was struggling to get his jacket on over the bulk. "Give it a rest, huh? You know my control is down when it's cold."

"This isn't cold, this is in the fifties."

"Yeah, well, it's cold when you're tryin' to throw strikes."

His father's reply came in sentences as crisp as burning leaves: "Excuses are all of equal value. They make us cowards. They deliver us from mental toughness."

"You think I'm makin' excuses."

"I *know* you're makin' excuses. The weather's the same for you as it is for everybody else."

The one thing Coley knew for sure was that his father wouldn't let go of this until he got the right answer. "What you want me to say is my right shoulder was flyin' open."

"It's not what I want you to say that matters. It's what you can learn that will help you improve."

"Okay, my right shoulder was flyin' open. The next time, I'll concentrate on it."

"The cold weather's only the excuse, yeah? It's the excuse to lose concentration. To lose mental toughness."

"Yeah, okay."

"What makes great pitchers is their concentration. They don't lose track of their mechanics even under adverse conditions. Besides which, it's not even cold out here."

"Yeah, okay, it's not cold." Coley was distracted as soon as he saw Bree Madison approaching the fence. She was wearing sunglasses. Her hair looked great, the way it blew in the breeze and radiated deep red color in the sun.

Now his father was asking him, "What about the times you had to cover first?"

"What?"

"Two times you covered first but you didn't follow the J route. You ran right at the bag as straight as a string."

"I got there, didn't I? I got the outs."

"Sometimes people get hits when they swing with their eyes closed," Ben Burke countered. "But you wouldn't expect them to do it consistently. Consistency comes from doing things the right way."

"Yeah, okay."

His father couldn't help noticing that he didn't have Coley's undivided attention. "I don't know who she is, but you suppose you could pay attention here for one more minute?"

Coley turned his gaze from Bree back to his dad. Ben Burke definitely knew the game. But these were old lectures and Coley wasn't in the mood to reprise them. "Did you notice I won the game?" he asked.

"Of course I noticed. I saw how you dominated Peoria Richwoods." When he said the words *Peoria Richwoods,* Ben's contempt was so evident he might have been talking about the girls' softball team.

"I dominated them without my good stuff," Coley added.

"Okay, you dominated them without your good stuff. Some people will be impressed by that, but it won't be you or me. That's not the next level."

"Okay, okay," said Coley, turning away. He saw Bree still waiting nearby, by herself. "I've got to go now."

"You go now. We can talk later."

Now, there's something to look forward to, Coley thought. He approached Bree so he could speak to her through the Cyclone fence. "How are you?" he asked her.

"I'm fine." She was smiling. "You were awesome."

"Nah. I didn't even have my good stuff."

"You were still awesome, though. They couldn't even get any hits."

"They had a couple. I'll have my good stuff when it gets hot, you wait and see. Are you a baseball fan?"

"I guess I could be," Bree answered.

Coley couldn't be sure what she meant by that, but it was a lot better listening to her compliments than to his father's criticism. Bree's fingers were hooked on to the fence. Her well-shaped fingernails were covered with a pale, frosted polish the color of cultured pearl. "Did you drive?" he asked her.

"You mean here? To the game?"

"Yeah, how'd you get here? Did you, like, drive or walk or what?"

"I don't have a license yet," she told him. "I'm only fifteen. I just stayed after school, until the game started." By extending her fingers, she was able to secure the hem of Coley's letter jacket in a tentative pincer grip. When she tugged, he let himself move flush against the fence.

"You want a ride home?"

"With you?" she asked. "You'd do that for me?" It was somewhat awkward through the fence, but she was in the process of fastening the bottom three snaps of his jacket. Deft as it was, it didn't happen quickly, because she had only the use of her fingers. No way to use her arms for leverage. She giggled as she went. It was a bold act of familiarity somehow, as intoxicating to Coley as it was unexpected. An unlikely combination of the maternal and the flirtatious.

He covered her fingers with his larger ones before he said, "I'll give you a ride. I have to get showered, but it won't take me long."

He tried to look into her eyes, but he saw instead his own image reflected in her sunglasses.

"Where should I meet you?" Bree asked him. She took off the shades to push some of the blowing hair from her face. At the corner of her left eye was a pale, greenish yellow blemish that looked like the final visible trace of a bruise. It wasn't eye shadow, though, that was plain. She wasn't wearing much makeup at all, except for the red lipstick, which was expertly applied.

Coley still covered her free hand with his own. "Just wait by my car in the parking lot. I'll be right out."

"It won't take you long, though, huh?"

"Not long at all. Ten minutes, tops."

"Okay, but promise it won't be more." She started to giggle.

"Okay, I promise." He turned to go, heading in the direction of the locker room, but after twenty feet or so he remembered to turn back. "My car's the purple Beretta."

"I know," he heard her say.

It took him eight minutes. His hair was still wet when he found her leaning against the passenger's side of the car, holding her books to her chest. As soon as she got in, Bree said, "This car is so cool."

Coley started the engine. "It's a good car except for the color."

"But I like the color."

"Who wants a purple car? My dad bought it out at Hennesy's because he got a great price on it. It was a program car."

"What's a program car?"

"It's like a demonstrator. Salesmen use them so people can make test drives."

Bree was twisting her torso in order to put her books in the backseat by way of the gap between the seats. Her short, silky skirt was one of those that buttoned down the front; it was high on her thighs. "But Coley, this is a *lavender* car, not a purple one. A purple car would be gross."

"Purple, lavender. Anyway, it's better than the last car I had."

"You had another car before this?"

"I've had two other cars. This is the third car I've had." Coley couldn't help wearing a sheepish grin while he delivered this information. They were idling by the stop sign at the entry to the street. "So you'll have to give me directions," he reminded her. "I don't know where your house is."

"Yale Boulevard. You know where it is?"

"I know." He pulled swiftly into the street and headed east on South Grand. Bree asked him if she could turn the rearview mirror in her direction, and he said, "No problem. I've got the side mirrors."

She began combing her hair. "Your dad buys you cars? You must be rich."

"We're rich enough," Coley had to admit. "I don't know who makes more money, though, my mom or my dad. She sells real estate."

Bree was still combing, leaning forward in her seat to get a better look in the mirror. "What car did you have before this?"

"It was a Honda Accord. It was okay, but it didn't have much guts. I talked my old man into getting this one."

"I think a lavender car is super cool." She was speaking to him, but by way of the mirror. Her legs weren't together and her skirt wasn't pulled down. She was arousing him, even if her suggestive body language wasn't premeditated. Maybe even *because* it wasn't.

"Lavender, purple."

Bree giggled before she said, "I'll take your old Honda when I turn sixteen, since you don't need it now."

"Sorry." He smiled. "It got traded in on this one." The left side of her face was less than a foot from his head. She was still combing the fine, straight hair with regular strokes, but it looked to him like everything was in place and there wasn't much more to accomplish. "How'd you get the bruise?" he asked casually. They were stopped at the Eleventh Street traffic light.

Before she answered, she put the sunglasses back on. "I hit it on the car door." She was putting the comb away in her purse.

"How did that happen?"

Something was different all of a sudden. Bree located herself squarely in her own seat. She crossed her legs and pulled the hem of her skirt down. "It just happened. It was clumsy. Don't ask so many questions."

"That was one question. If you don't want to talk about it, that's cool."

They were headed south on Eleventh Street. Bree was quiet. Content, it seemed, to stare out the passenger's window. Coley asked her about her family. She told him she lived with her mother and stepfather.

"Where does your real dad live?"

"He used to live in Texas. He still might, as far as I know. We practically never hear from him."

"What does your stepfather do?"

"He's a retired air force officer."

Coley didn't know much about her, but he decided she was a puzzle. The same girl who buttoned up his coat through the fence and gushed about his lavender car was now the one giving terse and reluctant answers to questions that didn't seem all that personal. He decided to change the subject. "So what do you say? You wanna go out? Let's go out to Knight's Action."

"I haven't been there. Is it nice?"

"Yeah. How about Friday?"

"I'm free on Friday," she said, "but what about Gloria?"

"I already told you. That's over."

She removed the sunglasses before turning to face him. "She's so popular, though."

Coley nodded. "That's good for her, then. She'll land on her feet."

"But I have to be sure," said Bree.

"You can be sure. Just trust what I'm tellin' you."

Bree's house was a modest Cape Cod on the east side of Yale Boulevard. She stood on the porch waving good-bye to him as he pulled away from the curb. The wind blew her hair and her skirt. Not too far from where she stood, a curtain was pulling back along the edge of the large picture window, but Coley couldn't see whose hand might be moving it.

Chapter Six

The next time Ruthie Roth brought him a notice in the library, Coley was set to be annoyed. He was reading the sports section of the *Tribune*. "What is it now?"

"You mean we have to stop meeting like this? Is that what you're saying?"

"Very funny. What do you want?"

Ruthie took the liberty of sitting in the closest chair, but she had to duck to avoid the wooden spindle on the spine of Coley's newspaper.

"Mrs. Alvarez wants to see you in her office," Ruthie informed him.

The box next to *immediately* had a check mark. Underneath, Mrs. Alvarez's signature was stamped in place. "I can see that," Coley said. "What the hell does she want?"

"How would I know? That would have to be between you and her."

Coley couldn't think what he might be in trouble for. His English midterm had come through; he wasn't flunking anything. At least he didn't *think* he was. Before he went to the office, he decided to ask Ruthie a favor. He asked her if she would help him with his values survey for human dynamics.

"You want me to help you with your homework."

She must have meant it as a question, even if it didn't sound like one. So he said, "Yeah, if you don't mind."

"Why should I mind? You're always there for me, aren't you?"

"If you're going to be sarcastic, then I take it back. Don't help me."

"Every time you need a favor, usually one that has to do with some class that's a problem for you, it's time for us to be friends."

"Oh, come on."

"Am I wrong, Coley?"

"You're exaggerating."

"Am I really? It seems the last time you wanted to associate with me was sophomore year, when I spent two weeks as your tutor for geometry. You were flunking, remember?"

He remembered. The fact he'd scraped by with a D was in no small part thanks to Ruthie. He probably would've flunked the final without the help. But he had to believe she was exaggerating.

"Okay, forget I even asked."

"Just like that? I should forget?"

Coley regretted he'd even brought it up. "You've got leftover makeup around your eyes. A little glitter, too, it looks like."

"It's theater makeup," she replied.

"Why do you need makeup for rehearsals?"

"I don't. But I like to experiment. Is that okay with you?"

Coley shrugged his shoulders. "If you want to look like a raccoon, it's okay with me." He took the newspaper back to the rack. When he returned, Ruthie stated, "Okay, I'll help you. But on one condition: You have to come to my house."

If this was meant as a challenge, Coley couldn't see it as one. "Fine."

"I may look like a raccoon, you never know."

"That's your call, Ruthie."

"I mean, I want you to be up front and visible about the fact that you're not afraid to spend time with me."

Now she was pissing him off. He picked up his books.

"That's bullshit, Ruthie, and you know it. Who am I supposed to be afraid of?"

"Oh. Did I forget I'm talking to Coley Burke? I should remember that you're one of the lucky few who go beyond the need for peer approval."

"Why don't you get going? You must have other people to annoy."

When he got to the office, Coley was relieved to find he wasn't in trouble. Mrs. Alvarez wanted help moving some boxes from the trunk of her car. "How did you know where to find me?" he asked her.

"I'm real smart that way, Coley. I know this is your study hall, and I know there aren't any magazines or sports pages in the auditorium."

"How long will this take?"

"Maybe ten minutes, fifteen at the most."

Coley shrugged. He didn't know why Mrs. Alvarez wanted him to be the box mover, but he said, "Okay, let's go."

Her car was in aisle H, so it was nearly a hundred yards from the front door of the school. A sharp wind was blowing. There were two boxes, about the same size, taped shut. Mrs. Alvarez told him one was light, full of tissue-paper balls that might be used at the prom. The other box, the one she wanted him to carry, was full of books.

"The prom is a long way off," Coley observed. "Why are you bringing decorations?"

"I needed the books, so why not bring the other things too? Makes one trip out of it."

The books were heavy, but he didn't complain. Before they got to the front door, he asked her if she'd spoken to Grissom about his book reports.

"Do you mean *Mrs.* Grissom?"

"That would be the one. Mrs. Grissom."

"Yes, I spoke to her. She said she has both of your reports but hasn't graded them yet."

Damn, he thought. *I need those grades.*

"And by the way, Coley, that other book you reported on? The one whose title you couldn't remember?"

"Yeah?"

"It was *The Old Man and the Sea,* by Ernest Hemingway."

"That sounds right." When they reached the front foyer door, Coley had to shift the heavy box onto a hip in order to toss the door open and hold it against the wind.

They were walking in the hallway, side by side. He noticed how, carrying a large box, Mrs. Alvarez seemed so small. "That's not a title many people forget," she went on. "That book's a classic."

"Why is this, like, an issue with you? I forgot the name of a book I read."

"Because I know a lot more about your academic history than I used to. I've been doing some investigating."

Oh, shit, Coley thought. As soon as they reached her office, he put his box on the floor next to the desk.

Mrs. Alvarez took her seat in the chair behind her desk. She told him, "You were a good student until the ninth grade."

Coley sat down in the chair across from her. It appeared they were going to have a conversation. "So?"

"So, then your grades started slipping. They still are."

"I'm probably not the first person that ever happened to."

"Probably not. Your brother, Patrick, on the other hand, was never a good student."

"How do you know all of this stuff?"

"I told you," said Mrs. Alvarez. "I've been doing some investigating. Student records are kept on the computer. They're not hard to find."

Coley didn't like the way this visit was developing. He sat up straighter in his chair. "Are there any more boxes to move, or are we done now?"

"We're done with boxes, but I'd really like to visit with you for a little while."

He was anxious to know what grades he might be getting on the two book reports. If he was good with those, he wouldn't have to worry about his baseball eligibility. He leaned back in his chair. "Okay," he finally said.

"Your brother died when you were in the ninth grade."

"That's true."

"That's when you started to slip."

She had Coley's attention. The way she said it made the dovetailing of the two things seem quite vivid. He told her quietly, "Mrs. Alvarez, you're the one with all the records. If you say it's true, I can't argue with it. What does it prove?"

"I'm not exactly sure if it proves anything, but it's interesting." She was cleaning her glasses. Every once in a while she held them up to the light for inspection.

"Okay, why is it, like, interesting?" Coley regretted the words almost as soon as he spoke them.

"I wonder if you've ever thought about guilt."

"Guilt?"

"When people die before their time," the counselor declared, "people close to them often feel guilty. Sometimes it's completely unreasonable. Maybe even most of the time it is. People often act out the guilt in roundabout ways."

"What ways? What guilt? I had nothin' to do with Patrick's death; he was wild and crazy. He got killed in a boating accident in Florida."

"I already told you it's not reasonable lots of times." She had her glasses back on and was looking straight at him.

Surprisingly, he found himself engaged in this give-and-take. He looked right back at her. "Did you feel guilty when your husband died?"

"Absolutely. I still do."

"Guilty about what?"

Mrs. Alvarez didn't waste time thinking about her answer. "He had to convince me that reenlisting in the service was a good thing for him to do. I probably could have talked him out of it."

This seemed to be getting very personal. "But he died in an accident, didn't he?"

"Yes. It was an accident."

"Mrs. Alvarez, that could've happened to him just driving a car or crossin' the street. None of it could be your fault."

"I know. I told you it wasn't reasonable." Her eyes glistened but didn't tear up.

"Okay, so why would I feel guilty about Patrick? Tell me something unreasonable about that."

"I have a theory, but that's all it is."

"So what's the theory?"

"Maybe you're afraid of too much success. What if your biggest fear is that you're better than Patrick?"

"Better in what way?"

"In any way. In every way."

"No offense, Mrs. Alvarez, but you're starting to sound like a shrink."

"I know." She reached down to drag the box of books in her direction. "But the fact remains, you were once a very good student and he never was. Based on the records I've

James W. Bennett

looked at, I'd say you're also a more generous person than he ever was."

The words *generous person* seemed like a description of a wuss. "Patrick had the fire and the killer instinct," he replied quickly.

"I don't doubt it. He was suspended from school at least four times. You've never been suspended from school; you don't even have a referral in your records."

"He was just a little bit wild and crazy, Mrs. Alvarez. He was fearless. That's one of the things that made him such a great pitcher. A great athlete, period. That was the quality that put him over the top."

She answered quietly, "That may also be the quality that put him in the grave, Coley. Based on the information I've gathered, I think that might be a fair statment, don't you?"

"Yeah, that too."

The counselor was taking paperback books from the box and stacking them on her desk. Coley asked her, "So how is this supposed to make me feel guilty? I'm a better *citizen* than Patrick and I used to be a better student. What's, like, the point?"

"What if you're a better baseball player than he was?"

"Say what?"

"What if you're simply superior to your older brother, even at baseball?"

"Mrs. Alvarez, that's crazy. You never saw Patrick pitch."

"That's true, I never did."

"He was on the Mets' roster by age twenty. He made the big club and was going to be heading north when they broke spring training. You never saw him pitch; he was awesome."

"Okay, he was awesome. If you think so, that's fine."

"What's up with that—*if I think so?*"

"I mean, if you really think so, that's fine." She was speaking softly. Her sincerity was never more evident. "On the other hand, if you were better than Patrick, how would that make you feel?"

"This is too crazy. This is nuts."

"Maybe, but why not answer the question? How would it make you feel?"

"I have no idea."

"Would it kill you to think about it?"

"Why? What would be the point?"

"Your older brother is your measuring stick. If you surpass him, what does that do to you? How does it affect the things you do and the choices you make? That would be the point."

Coley let out a deep sigh. *I came here to carry some books for her and now this.* "Mrs. Alvarez, this is all over my head."

"That's exactly what I'm talking about. That's the easy way out, isn't it? That's what feels safe." But she was smiling.

Coley looked at the clock. It was four minutes till passing period. "I'd better get back," he said. "I've got world history."

She was still smiling. It was a warm smile indeed. "Just bear with me another minute. I didn't ask you to carry these books inside for no reason. Some of them are for you."

She pushed six paperbacks across the desk in his direction. They were all in good condition. One was called *A Portrait of the Artist as a Young Man.* The only one he'd ever heard of was *Catcher in the Rye.*

He had to smile. "Why are you giving me books?"

"These books belonged to Hector," replied the counselor. "I've been sorting through some of his things."

Sifting through the possessions of a dead husband was a sobering notion; Coley couldn't respond right away. "Your husband had books?"

"Lots and lots of books. I picked these out for you because I thought they might be appropriate. If not right now, then later, when you're in college."

Coley appreciated her thoughtfulness but felt the need to be honest. "You know I'm not much good in English, Mrs. Alvarez."

"I know you're not much good in English *now*. You're an underachiever, but I think we've established that you're not stupid."

"I've never been much of a book reader, though." As best he could remember, the only book he'd read on his own within the past year was Tom Seaver's book on pitching mechanics.

"Maybe you will be someday," she replied. "A book reader, that is."

It was hard for Coley to imagine such a development, but this wasn't a time for arguing. "It's real nice of you, Mrs. Alvarez, thanks."

"Hector loved baseball. He saw you pitch a couple of times when you were a sophomore. I think it would please him to know that some of his books ended up in your hands." Her eyes glistened when she spoke this last sentence.

"Thanks," he said again. Then he added, "I think you're looking for a way to improve my mind."

"I'm just hoping you'll find a way to put more of your mind to use."

"That would be the same thing, though, wouldn't it? I mean, the more you use a thing, the stronger it gets, like a lifting program to strengthen your arms and legs."

"I suppose. Now get on out of here—go to world history. I need to get some work done today."

Coley took the books to his locker before he returned to the library.

For his birthday Coley got his own credit card. Visa Gold. His dad got a new lawn tractor, the top-of-the-line John Deere, all shiny green with a huge mowing deck. It was parked in the driveway, where Ben Burke sat high in the saddle, leafing through the owner's manual.

"For Coley's birthday you bought yourself a lawn tractor?" asked his mother sarcastically.

"It will benefit him, too. It'll mean he'll have to spend less time on yard work."

"Oh, please. Since when did anyone other than Trinh do any yard work around here? Besides me, I mean."

Coley knew how right she was. The only chores he or his father did around the house were touch and go. They hired Trinh for all the heavy lifting.

"This is just a toy," his mother said.

"But it's a toy I don't have," his father pointed out.

"Not true. You already have a tractor."

"*Had* a tractor. I traded it in on this one."

"The fact remains, it's Coley's birthday, not yours."

His dad lobbied his position by saying, "I've been trying to tell you how he'll be a beneficiary. So will Trinh. I'd say it's a win-win proposition."

"I'd say it's a dramatic lesson in credit card abuse." She turned to Coley to add, "This is called impulse buying. People with credit cards are prone to this kind of behavior."

His dad said, "I paid cash for this tractor," but his mother paid no attention. She continued speaking to Coley: "There's a giddy freedom that sometimes goes with plastic purchasing. People buy things they don't need, with money they don't have."

Dad concurred, keeping a straight face: "Your mother's right, Son. It can be a demon for sure. A credit card demands a lot of personal responsibility."

Coley found it almost entertaining when his parents argued this way. Toothless and scripted, it seemed like an old shoe, so absent of malice it was more like a workout than a quarrel. If it was an argument about Patrick, though, he knew how down and dirty it could get. *Would* get.

He went up to his father's study to play back phone messages, but there were none for him. He received birthday cards from two major-league organizations, the White Sox and the Texas Rangers. He wondered how he could see this credit card as an asset; hadn't his parents' plastic always been available to him when he needed it?

The day the tulip tree started to bloom behind the third-base bleachers was the day Coley pitched his first no-hitter of the season, in a game against Eisenhower. He had pitched four no-hitters as a junior, so this was nothing unique.

Nevertheless, it wasn't pretty, nor was it altogether satisfying. It took him three innings to really find his rhythm, by which time Eisenhower had scored two runs on a combination of walks and throwing errors. In the end Coley walked five but he struck out thirteen.

A fifth-inning throwing error by Rico Cates was premeditated, designed to save the no-hitter. But it nearly led to another run. When one of the Eisenhower batters hit a high hopper back toward the mound, it was slightly to Coley's left side and too high for him to reach. He leaped as high as he could but couldn't grab it; he was pretty sure the ball had grazed the tip of his glove.

The ball was bouncing feebly between the mound and second base when Rico swooped in to barehand it. He unleashed a hopelessly wild, off-balance throw that sailed at least ten feet over the first baseman's head and landed beyond the restraining fence.

"You think you coulda got him?" Coley asked his shortstop.

"No way," said Rico. "Not even if I was Derek Jeter. Nohow.

Let's just hope the throw was shitty enough they give me an error."

Coley couldn't help laughing. "Thanks, amigo."

"No problem. You do what you have to do." By this time the umpire had given Coley a new ball and was telling them to break up the socializing.

"Now you got to strike the next two guys out," Rico reminded him, "or this dude here might score."

"No sweat, I've got my rhythm now." He struck out the next two batters to end the inning. Nobody reached base against him in the final two innings.

Even his father was impressed. "You worked a good game, Son, once you got your rhythm."

"Thanks," Coley mumbled.

"The next step is, find your rhythm from the get-go. That's called consistent focus."

"Consistent focus," Coley murmured.

"Richie Romine was here today," his father continued.

"Who's Richie Romine?"

"He's a scout for the Expos. He was sitting over there by the phone booth for the last four innings."

"I didn't know there were any scouts here."

"That's always the best situation, isn't it? If you know scouts are around, it can be a distraction."

Chapter Seven

Right from the start Coley didn't like Burns, who was Bree's father. Or rather, stepfather. Maybe it was the way he took your space by getting too close for comfort when he talked to you. He was a big man, too, at least six feet two inches and heavily muscled. An inch or more shorter than Coley, but maybe ten pounds heavier.

Even when he told Coley he'd heard he was a terrific pitcher, he was still maintaining the handshake and standing with his face about eighteen inches away. It might have been meant as a compliment, but something about his demeanor suggested challenge. His beer breath was too close.

Bree's mother seemed timid in the extreme. She made a brief appearance near the sofa to say she was pleased to meet him, then returned to the kitchen table, where she had a game of solitaire in progress.

Burns had a fleshy, youngish face, with only the well-defined creases at the corners of his eyes to suggest he was over forty. His crew cut, even though it had some gray in it, added to his youthful appearance. He said to Coley, "You can have her back no later than eleven, then."

"No problem," Coley answered. They had already confirmed this a few moments earlier.

Then he was in close again; he seemed to keep his eyes locked on for a second or two too long. "We'll leave the light on for you."

By the time they got to the car, Coley felt relieved. He was driving his mother's Chrysler because it had the bench seat, which would give Bree the chance to sit close. She did. Had she squirmed any closer, she would have been perched in his lap. It was sure as hell a much more promising package of body language than what her old man delivered.

Coley started the car. He felt inclined to say something about the stepfather, but he didn't want to sound negative. He settled on, "He sure seems awful young to be retired."

"That's the way it is when you're in the service," Bree told him. "You can retire after twenty years, so you might only be forty or forty-five."

"I guess that's cool."

"Not really. It gives him too much time around the house. About the only thing he ever does is play golf." The left side of her arm was making full contact against him.

From time to time, when she let her hand fall briefly on his thigh, the swelling in his groin caused him to shift his hips carefully. He was wearing his blue jeans, but Bree had on a pair of low-slung, hip-hugging pink pants and a matching string halter top. On her feet were white patent leather thong sandals. It didn't surprise Coley when she tilted the rearview mirror so she could give her hair a close inspection.

"You changed your do," Coley observed.

"It's a teased ponytail. It's the first time I ever tried it. Do you like it?"

He wasn't sure if he liked it or not, but he did enjoy the generous side view of her tits that the skimpy halter top allowed. He had to remind himself to watch the traffic. "It's real nice, Bree."

She spoke to the mirror: "It's kind of hard to do, but it's one of the best ponytails there is for girls who don't have real long hair.

You have to spritz some hair spray on your roots, and then work it back with a teasing comb."

It was more hair-care detail than Coley needed. "It looks real nice," he said again.

"You like it, don't you?"

"I like it."

"I'm going to let my hair grow real long so I can do it in a French twist down the back. You can even make a croissant-shaped tail that way."

They were in the parking lot at Knight's Action by this time and out of the car. Bree was childlike and spirited on the miniature golf course. She jumped for joy when she made a putt, but hopped her frustration up and down when she missed. She disregarded her hair even when it started coming loose at its barrette, and she had so much flesh on display, Coley could only think how much he ached to get her in the sack.

They stopped at the concession building briefly for a soft drink. As soon as they left, they found themselves headed in the direction of the batting cages. "I feel like a few swings," Coley told her. "You wanta hit a few?"

"I don't know anything about hitting baseballs."

"There's one machine that has real slow pitches. Are you sure?"

"I'm sure. You can hit balls if you want."

"Just a few swings," he said.

"I'll just watch while I finish my Coke," Bree said. She followed him toward the cages, fussing with her hair again.

Most of the cages were in use, but one near the end was available. Had he been by himself or with Rico, he would have selected the 90 mph option; but under these conditions, with Bree watching, he decided to make a better impression. Coley chose the medium mode, which brought the pitch at about 78 mph, 80 at the most.

He put in two dollars' worth of quarters, but it took several swings before he felt relaxed. After that he felt comfortable; he began making solid contact and driving the ball consistently.

They walked hand in hand past the small swimming pool where the Disney figures were positioned among some stacked vinyl recliners. The water recreational facilities wouldn't be open for several weeks yet. "I didn't know you were such a good hitter," said Bree.

"It's not a big deal to hit against a pitching machine," Coley replied. He was glad she was impressed, though. "A pitching machine is so consistent there's no stress when you hit against it."

"But you really know how to clobber that ball. I thought you were just a pitcher."

"I used to be a good hitter. I could be again if I ever worked at it, but I concentrate on pitching about ninety percent of the time."

"Are you going to be in the big leagues?"

It was naive the way she asked the question. "I'd like to be; I guess I've got a chance. It's what my old man wants, that's for sure."

"Does he, like, put pressure on you?"

"You could call it that. If he was here and he saw me hitting in the cage, he'd want to know if I learned anything about pitching. When it comes to baseball, there's no such thing as just doing it for fun."

They were following the path that rounded the water slide. Bree changed the subject. "I have to get a new suit for summer."

"You mean a swimsuit?"

"Yeah. I saw this string bikini at Kohl's last week. It was kind of turquoise."

"You'd have the guts to wear it?"

Bree tossed her head before she said, "Why not? I look good in bikinis."

Coley didn't doubt it. "I'm sure you do. That's not what I meant."

"I'd probably have to get a bikini wax, though."

"Oh, God."

"Why do you say that?"

"Because it's nuts what girls will do to their own body, just for the sake of fashion."

"I don't think it is. I mean, if you're going to, like, get your legs waxed, it's no big deal to have a bikini wax, too."

"Whatever." Coley didn't feel like arguing, and he wasn't sure how he'd hold up his end of a conversation about Bree's pubes. "What about *your* father?" he asked her.

"You mean Burns. He's not my father, he's my *step*father. What about him?"

"Okay, what's he like?"

"Why are you asking me this?"

"You asked me about my old man, so I thought maybe I'd ask about yours. I think it's called conversation."

"I hate him," said Bree. She turned away when she said it.

"Hate? Isn't that, like, pretty strong? Why do you hate him?"

"I told you, you're not supposed to ask me so many questions."

"That's just one question, for Christ's sake."

But she was running by this time, past the smaller water slide, across the abbreviated boardwalk that fronted the bumper boat area, and along the lakeside path where the paddleboats were moored. The light was dim there, but Coley could still see her. Her running form was good, but she looked so small from this distance. Perplexed, he followed her. Walking, though, not running.

She was headed for the picnic pavilion, which was deserted.

Since she hadn't been to Knight's Action Park before, Coley wondered how she knew where she was going. If, indeed, she did.

Bree was turning herself in circles by hugging one of the iron poles that supported the roof, like a child swinging on a playground apparatus. It was dark in the pavilion; some of the picnic tables, stacked on end like dominoes, made a partial shield against the pale light that might have reached them from the parking lot.

She came near to him as soon as Coley took a seat on the edge of one of the tables that were level. She planted several brief, playful kisses on his chin and eyes. Then she moved her mouth on his and thrust her tongue inside.

She astonished him. *Who is she?* he wondered while he swallowed as much of her active tongue as he could. "I hear she's hot," Rico had reported. When they broke the seal, he asked her, "I thought you said you didn't like to mess around."

"I have my moments," she said. "I have to be sure."

"You have to be sure of what?"

"I mean, I have to be sure of you."

"I don't understand."

"Maybe not now, but maybe you will." She was looking straight into his eyes. "You're so big, aren't you?"

"What do you mean, 'so big'?"

"I mean, I can hardly get my arms clear around you." Bree was running her fingertips slowly down both sides of his face. Coley shivered slightly, not so much from the cool night air as with desire. He pulled her close roughly to kiss her again. He was aroused and he wanted her. His fingers were just below her shoulder blades, where the string of her halter top made a horizontal path across her lean rib cage. He was tentative, as all this was happening faster than he had expected. He untied the string slowly, waiting for the resistance that never came.

JAMES W. BENNETT

Bree stepped back from him again, this time about two feet. Her top, even though loosed from its bottom anchor, still hung to cover most of her chest. While his large hands rested on her waist, she reached behind her neck to untie the bow at the top. Looking him straight in the eye, and smiling, she asked him, "Is this what you want?" She let the halter top drop. It landed on his knees.

Bree was using her folded arms to conceal her freed-up breasts. "You like?" she asked him.

"Who wouldn't?" he asked her back. Coley was staring at her dumbly, with a dry mouth. Even though he was experienced with girls, he had never been gifted with a gesture this bold or seductive. You would only expect it from movies or television shows, if you would expect it at all.

She held him tight around the neck while his fingers worked the slick flesh of her naked back. He longed for a better look at her breasts; the modesty of her body language had permitted only the briefest view of their shape and definition, and only then in the poorest light. But each time he tried to separate himself, she simply clamped him tighter, giggling all the while.

"I want to look," he whispered. He was letting his tongue caress her earlobe.

"Do you?"

"Yeah, I need to see."

"You don't want much, do you?" she teased. Her grip was still tight. Coley was surprised her thin arms could generate so much strength. He could have forced them apart, but no way would that be cool.

He used his teeth to tug gently at her earlobe. "I don't have a condom," he said.

This remark only provoked her to more giggling. "It doesn't matter anyway," she whispered. "This is as far as we go."

"Oh, man, you serious?" He felt the keen edge of frustration and disappointment. He was so hard his too-tight blue jeans were cramping him. He wanted her, and he wanted her now.

"There'll be other nights," she explained.

"You never can tell. There are no guarantees in life."

"True enough." She released her grip to step back, but she kept her arms folded across her chest. "I think we'd better go."

Was her smile a promise of some kind, or merely simple mischief? "Let's stay a little longer, Bree."

"It's after ten thirty."

"We won't be late even if we stay a little longer." The curfew imposed by her stepfather was unfamiliar and frustrating. Her folded arms were creating a lot of pushed-up cleavage but obstructing the view and access he craved.

"I'm serious, though," she said. "We have to."

"We don't really."

"I said we do." She wasn't smiling anymore. She turned away and wriggled back into the halter top with her back turned. She tied the bows swiftly. "I thought you didn't like to mess around," said Coley.

"You said that before. I told you I have my moments."

"You're not a tease, are you?"

"I'm sure I don't know what you mean by that." Now she was facing him again. "Let's just say I'm trying to give you something to look forward to," she said with a provocative smile.

The week he was intimate with Bree for the first time was also the week Coley pitched the perfect game. Well, almost; it was perfect for the length of time he pitched.

They made love on his bed, after practice, when the house was empty. Bree's lean body might have suggested adolescence, but

JAMES W. BENNETT

there was nothing juvenile about her manner of participation in the sex act. She was as focused and fearless in the pursuit of her passion as any grown woman. Since she was only fifteen, Coley wanted to believe in her innocence, but it wouldn't be easy. In the heat of the moment he didn't even remember to use a condom.

The game against Urbana, which came two days later, was his best of the year. He was grooved from the first pitch, in the warm spring air. It didn't seem likely that the passion he had explored with Bree could be linked to this overpowering performance on the mound, and yet somehow it did. It was a day when he was a man among boys, and there was something about his relationship with her that made him feel like a man.

Coley struck out the side in the first and third innings. He might have done the same in the fourth but for a feeble pop-up to deep short.

His fastball, which was clocked consistently at 92 and 93 mph on his father's JUGS gun, and a time or two at 94, had movement and location. He threw his slider now and again not because he needed it to get people out, but simply to work on spotting it in the strike zone. The Urbana batters were completely overmatched; when they got swings at all, they were usually the feeble kind. He was ahead in the count so consistently that he was almost never in danger of walking anyone.

At the end of five innings Coley knew he was pitching a perfect game. So did Coach Mason, as well as his teammates. Everyone followed the time-honored rule of not talking about it; nobody wanted to cast a jinx.

Coley could see Bree sitting in the bleachers, not too far from where his parents were located. He knew there were major-league scouts as well, but his indifference to them helped establish a pressure-free condition. He poured live fastballs over the corner with so little effort he felt like he was ready to take on the Atlanta Braves. He couldn't remember being zoned like this before; it was practically euphoric. Each batter might just as well have been the motionless statue of Reggie Jackson in the backyard. Paralyzed. Just bodies with bats, taking up space until it was their turn to drag on back to the bench.

But then in the top of the seventh, with his team leading 6-0, it happened. Just two outs away from finishing his masterpiece. An Urbana hitter topped a lame grounder to the right of Ricky Huff, the first baseman. Coley needed to cover first, but he was too slow to react. When he did remember, he ran fast, but he had to make a beeline straight at the bag instead of the preferred J route.

He meant to come down with his foot on the base, but Huff's throw was enough behind him to throw him off stride. When he reached back for the ball, he lost his rhythm and stumbled over the bag. He rolled his ankle severely on the edge of the hard base and somewhat forward, just before he fell into the dirt in foul territory.

He couldn't recall some crucial details, like did he hold the ball and did he beat the runner to first? But he knew right away, the way he had snapped himself, that the injury was severe. The knowledge came first, before the pain. It came before the state of shock and the nausea. To have the knowledge didn't seem fair somehow—wouldn't the pain itself be enough suffering? He used his elbows to try to drag himself in the direction of the team bench.

He couldn't go far, though. By the time the furious pain in his ankle began its radiating path throughout other parts of his body, he was on his back. Blocking out the sky were the faces of his teammates, Coach Mason, and Odoms, the trainer on loan from the university. Coley wished they would all vanish so he could just throw up; the nausea came right in tandem with the cold sweats.

Odoms was breaking open his case to get an ice pack. While he wrapped it gingerly around the ankle (it was the right one) with a fresh ACE bandage, Coley closed his eyes. He tried taking deep, regular breaths, but they didn't come easy. He opened his eyes to discover that the faces of his parents had been added to the group. His father worked his jaw but didn't speak. Coley knew why: He wanted to know the extent of the injury before any such information was available. His concern about the pain and discomfort would come after.

"Get me that blanket," he heard Coach Mason say.

"Don't move, man," he heard Rico say. "Just lay still."

Then Jamie Quintero said, "Yeah. Just lay still."

Coach repeated himself, "Where the hell's the blanket? I said somebody get me that blanket."

The words his mother spoke were, "Has anyone called an ambulance?"

Coley had to get x-rayed at the hospital before any plan of treatment was considered. By the time he was in the X-ray room itself, the symptoms of shock and nausea were diminishing. There wasn't much solace from this development, however. It only gave him room to concentrate on the acute pain in the ankle, which seemed to intensify with each passing minute.

The ER physician was a woman named Sloan. She removed the ice pack from Coley's elevated ankle so she could begin to probe the swollen damage with her fingertips. The pain was so intense a couple of times that Coley nearly cried out.

"The good news," Dr. Sloan explained, "is that nothing's broken. The X rays are negative."

"Okay," said Coley's father, "what's the bad news?"

"The bad news is that nothing's broken."

"Are you trying to be funny?"

"Not really." The doctor was looking at the ankle closely while speculating out loud. "It's a major sprain, that's for sure. It may have to be put in a cast, but it's too soon to tell."

"A cast?"

"Maybe. We can't know that for a few days, or until this swelling goes down enough to reexamine it."

"Are you talking about a hard cast?" Ben Burke wanted to know. "As in plaster of paris?"

"Maybe so, maybe fiberglass. The material's not really an issue, but there's internal bleeding here and ligament damage. The question is, how severe is it?"

"I hate to butt in," said Coley impatiently, "but this thing here hurts like hell." He was pointing at the ankle.

"No doubt," said Dr. Sloan. "I'll send some pain pills home with you."

"Let me get this straight," said Dad firmly. "You're getting ready to send him home, but you're talking about putting his ankle in a cast?"

"We're talking about a lot of things," said Dr. Sloan with a smile. She pushed her glasses up so they sat firmly on the bridge of her nose. "And most of it's premature. That's my point. The goal over the next forty-eight to seventy-two hours is to limit internal bleeding and reduce swelling." She was speaking to Coley now. "You need to keep icing your ankle until it starts to feel numb, then take it off. That usually takes in the neighborhood of twenty minutes. When you feel it warming up again, repeat the process."

"Even at night?"

"No, you have to sleep at night. You have ACE bandages at home?"

Coley nodded.

"Wrap the ankle in one of those when you go to bed. Compress

James W. Bennett

it. Try to sleep with the ankle elevated by using pillows to get it above your hips."

Coley shifted his weight in order to get on his side. "What about walking?"

The doctor was shaking her head. "You can't put any weight on it before it's reexamined. You'll be on crutches for a while, my friend."

"No offense," said Coley's father, "but are you a specialist, Dr. Sloan? Are you an expert in orthopedics or sports medicine?"

"Nope, I'm just your basic ER sawbones." Saying this, Dr. Sloan returned her stethoscope to her ears and began listening to Coley's heart. Coley had to wonder if this was really necessary, or if it was the doctor's way of screening Dad out.

"Because," Coley's father persisted, "we're going to need a second opinion on this. There's no way for you to know it, but this happens to be a crucial time in this boy's life."

Dr. Sloan took the stethoscope from her ears before she said, "I think that's an excellent idea." The doctor's demeanor showed that she was annoyed but in control. "Mr. Burke, what I'm trying to tell you is that you don't even have a *first* opinion yet. The procedure I've outlined is simply to get you to that point. In two or three days, when the swelling is reduced, I suggest you take him to the sports medicine clinic in Champaign."

"No offense, okay?"

"No offense at all."

The Darvocet pills Coley took smothered the pain, but they also put him in the fitful sleep that activated dreams. Some of the dreams were about Bree and some were about his brother, Patrick. They seemed to be rooted in actual events but embroidered with preposterous details.

His mother came down the first morning to ask him how the ankle was.

"It hurts like hell. I'm going to take some more of those pain pills."

"Don't overdo that," she cautioned him. "Just take them if you have to."

"They put me to sleep and they give me dreams. You don't have to worry about the ankle, though. I'll be okay."

His mother smiled without parting her lips. "I'm not about to worry about another sports injury, with all we've had in this house."

That had to be the truth. Coley remembered the time Patrick played a whole football game with his broken hand in a soft cast.

"I've made up twelve of these," his mother told him, holding up a Ziploc baggie full of ice cubes. "They're in the freezer."

"Are you going to bring my breakfast down too?" *Fat chance.*

"I think you know me better than that," was the answer. "You need help, but you don't need a servant."

Coley peeled back the Velcro strips that secured the plastic ankle splint so he could apply the ice cubes. "Thanks anyway, Ma. For the ice, I mean."

"Don't call me Ma. Are you going to school today?"

"Not today."

"How about tomorrow?"

"Not tomorrow, either."

"Is that your decision, or your father's?"

"He doesn't want me to take any chances. On the stairs, or whatever. I haven't practiced much on the crutches yet. If it was up to me, I'd rather go to school." Saying so, Coley thought of Bree. Maybe she could come over after school and help with the business of nursing him back to health.

"If it were up to you," said his mother, repeating his own words but lacing them with innuendo. She took a seat on the edge of his bed and stared out the only window, which was just above ground level.

"Yeah. If it were up to me. I don't want to get caught in the middle of this, Mother."

"Better me than you, Coley? Is that what you're trying to say?"

"You know that's not what I mean either."

"That's the story of our family, isn't it? Caught in the middle?"

He knew what she was getting at. If she wasn't caught in the middle, then he himself was. "Except for Dad," he said.

His mother looked at him. "He may be caught in the middle more than either one of us," she said.

"*Him?* How?"

"Between sons," was her quick reply.

"That's too much to think about. My head hurts."

His mother was wearing the white ruffled blouse and the beige pleated skirt. She had on her high-heeled shoes. Before she left the house, she would put on the gold blazer with her name tag, then go sell houses. She would make lots of money doing it, but Coley had to believe that if she stopped getting paid, she wouldn't take much notice of the fact. She would probably go right on making appointments and showing houses.

Maybe I should talk to her, he thought. *Maybe I should talk to her more.* "I've been having dreams," he told her. "One of them was about Patrick."

"Maybe it's the medication."

"Yeah, I think maybe it is."

"So tell me about the Patrick dream."

"It was a dream about the time I went to visit him in Florida at the spring training complex. In the dream he was fixing me up with these beautiful chicks." *Hoping to get me laid,* Coley thought without saying so out loud.

His mother turned to look at him. "Is that what happened when you went to Florida?"

"No, that's not what happened."

"He didn't fix you up with *chicks*?" She spoke the word like an expletive.

"Of course not. I'm talkin' about a dream. The facts were, he let me throw some in the complex, I even got to take a little batting practice. You should've seen all the kids hangin' around and the way they envied me. At night he usually had dates or parties and stuff, but he gave me the key to his hotel room so I could watch HBO. One night he bought me tickets for this amusement park that was only a couple miles away."

"That would be better than fixing you up with chicks, wouldn't it?"

Her sarcasm was annoying. "I'm just trying to make conversation," he said. "I had a good time in Florida."

"And why not? You got to watch HBO every night."

"Look, why are you dissin' Patrick like this, anyway? I said I *dreamed* he was fixin' me up; it didn't really happen."

"It just sounds like something he would do," replied his mother matter-of-factly.

"Oh, get real."

His mother returned her gaze toward the window before she said, "Patrick used to throw the neighbor's cat back into their yard by the tail. They called the cops on us."

"Big deal. Maybe they needed to keep their cat where it belonged."

"When he went to summer camp, they sent him home because he insisted on dunking people in the swimming pool."

"Yeah, well, I got sent home from summer camp too," Coley said without thinking.

"That was completely different. You got sent home from camp because you were homesick, not because you were tormenting other people."

"What are you tryin' to say?" Coley hated the fact that his own slip of the tongue had resurrected the humiliating memory of getting homesick at summer camp.

"What I'm trying to say is that Patrick had a nasty streak. At times it was more than a streak. Nobody ever talks about it much because he was such a sports star."

"No, you've got it wrong. Patrick was just mentally tough. That's the thing that set him apart."

"That's certainly what the sports pages always said."

"I don't know what you're tryin' to say here, but I can do without it."

"So can I," agreed his mother. She was getting to her feet. "I came down to find out about your ankle, not to get into an argument about Patrick. I'll be home for lunch. You can let me know if you need any books or homework from school."

"Yeah, okay."

Chapter Eight

The assessment of Coley's injury at the sports medicine clinic was no more encouraging than the one from the emergency room. It was a Dr. Nugent this time, who explained that the ankle would have to be in a hard cast for two to three weeks.

"Jesus Christ," said Coley.

"Not good news, I know." Coley's X rays were up on the wall in front of a bright screen. "This is somewhere between a grade two and a grade three sprain, which means it's moderate to severe. You've torn the fibers in the ligaments that cover the outside of your ankle." Dr. Nugent was seated on a tall stool while he spoke, aiming a pointer in the direction of the X rays.

But Coley had more interest in the bottom line than in the pictures on the wall. "I need to pitch," he said.

"You need to get well first," countered the doctor.

"But I need to *pitch*," Coley insisted.

Dr. Nugent smiled. It was obvious he'd had this conversation with injured athletes before. "You don't just need to pitch, you need to pitch well. That won't happen unless this injury is completely healed and then you take it through proper rehab. You with me?"

Coley closed his eyes and rubbed them. He couldn't believe what he was hearing. A sprained ankle? He'd had them before but been back in action in just a few days. "Jesus Christ," he said again. "How much time are we talkin' here?"

"Worst-case scenario, two months. A month in the cast followed by a month of systematic rehab."

"In two months our season will be over," said Coley glumly.

"There's a wonderful thing about being eighteen," said Dr. Nugent with another smile. "There are so many seasons left."

Cute, Coley thought. From the corner of his eye he could see his father working his jaw. He wanted to give the old man credit for keeping his mouth shut, but his excruciating pattern of toe wagging and rubber band snapping had the effect of breaking the silence.

Coley sighed before he asked Dr. Nugent, "Okay, what's the best-case scenario?"

"That would be two weeks in the cast and two weeks in rehab."

"And then I could pitch again?"

"Only a couple of innings to start with. You have to remember, you won't be in shape; you aren't going to be doing any running for at least a month."

Coley was trying, by the numbers, to put the best face on this. "If I could pitch in a month, that's still before the play-offs. Maybe I could be in shape for the play-offs."

"Maybe. But you have to remember, that would be best case scenario. When we talk in these best- and worst-case terms, we're talking about the extremes that might develop. Reality usually falls somewhere in between."

"We have a good chance to make state," Coley informed him. "We could even win it."

"I know," said Dr. Nugent.

"You do?"

"Yes. I read the sports pages."

For the first time Coley's father spoke up. He wanted to know when they should come back.

"Let's be optimists," replied Dr. Nugent. "Let's take the cast off in two weeks and reexamine the ankle at that time. No promises, though."

"Will there be any permanent damage?" Ben Burke asked him.

"There shouldn't be, not if he goes strictly by the book in his rehab."

On the drive home Coley tried to make his right leg and ankle comfortable by tilting his seat back. It didn't work; all he was doing was causing pain by stretching his groin muscles awkwardly.

The quarrel began when his father looked for the silver lining. He said, "At least you can still lift."

Bored by this observation, Coley replied, "I can still lift."

"With the extra time you can lift even more than you have been."

"Now, there's somethin' to look forward to."

"Don't be a smart-ass. Just because you can't run doesn't mean you have to stop strengthening your upper body."

Coley thought of Bree. *I didn't realize you were so big; it's hard to reach my arms around you.* It was the first pleasant thought he'd had all day. He said, "I'm two hundred fifteen pounds, Pa, and it's all muscle. I'm not exactly skin and bones in my upper body."

"You know what I'm saying, and don't call me Pa. The second thing is, you'll have more time for homework."

"That's even better than liftin' weights. Why should I be bummed at all?"

"Don't be a smart-ass," his father said again.

"I'm okay with my grades."

"You are? Not according to Mrs. Alvarez. She sent us a note that you got a progress report in English."

"Why the hell did she do that? I explained it all to her."

"You're on the bubble in English."

"I'm not on the bubble. Grissom turned in the report before

she read my book summaries. I explained all that to Alvarez. Why the hell did she send you a note?"

"Because she doesn't have any choice, that's why. If she gets a progress report from a teacher, she's required to notify the parents."

"Jesus Christ."

"You're swearing too much these days. It wouldn't hurt you to clean up your act. Anyway, how many times do I have to lay it out for you? With your ACT scores, you can't get less than a C in any of your classes."

"I know, I know. If I want to keep the baseball scholarship I can't get less than a 2.3. How many times do we have to go through this?"

"Until you *act* like you know, I guess. And you have to get at least one B. Where's the B going to come from?"

Human dynamics, Coley thought. But his frustration had escalated too far to talk about it. "Can you get off my case? Isn't it bad enough I have this ankle?"

"The ankle's the whole point. Bobby Esau saw you pitch the game you got injured. He thinks you're ready. He thinks you'll go high in the major-league draft."

"I know. And he's not the only one. Who the hell needs college anyway?"

"That may be your only good option, because of the ankle. If the pros think you're damaged goods, if they don't see something more out of you again this spring, they'll probably back off."

"I'll pitch good again before the season's over."

"Maybe. *Maybe* you will, but you can't predict that. The point is, nobody can take a scholarship away unless you don't qualify academically."

Coley's back hurt. He flipped the lever to maneuver his seat into the upright position. He moved his ankle to the side before he said, "This is just great. The ankle knocks me out of the major-league draft, or Grissom's English class knocks me out of the scholarship."

"Stop whining, for God's sake. There's nothing on your plate that you can't handle."

This rebuke made Coley feel like a child. "Are we done now?" he asked.

"Done with what?" questioned his father.

"With this conversation. It sucks."

"I guess we can be done."

"Good." Coley thought of Bree and wondered if he would see her tonight.

It was two days later, and Bree didn't bother knocking. She simply let herself in the front door and then bounced her way down the steps. Coley, who was lifting weights, hadn't heard her enter the house. *Oprah* was on.

Bree had a box of cookies, which she'd baked herself. She gave him one, then another, and then a third. Chocolate chip. He devoured them rapidly. "You bake these?"

"Yes, I know how to bake cookies. Don't they say the way to a man's heart is through his stomach?"

"That's not the way I heard it, Bree. I heard it was through something else."

She laughed and then teased him, "Ooooh, Coley. You're not going to be bad, are you? I'm here on an errand of mercy; are you going to be bad?"

"Not me," he replied.

"Oh, I love Oprah. Isn't it awful boring lifting weights?"

"Boring as hell."

"Are you glad to see me?"

"What do you think?"

"Are your parents home?"

"Nobody's home. It's just you and me, babe."

Bree giggled. "Maybe we can find something more interesting for you to do."

"Let's hope." Coley was flat on his back on the vinyl weight bench, wearing an ancient tank top that said SARASOTA and a pair of fleece gym shorts. "How'd you get here?" he asked her.

"Rico brought me. He said he can even drive me home if I need him to." She took off her sweater. She was wearing a sleeveless blouse and a miniskirt. The skirt flared even higher when she spun to lay the box of cookies on the entertainment center.

"We don't need Rico," Coley said. "I can drive you home." He had the weight bench adjusted so his feet could reach the floor on both sides. He didn't use his feet for weight bearing, but their contact with the floor gave him the proper leverage for bench pressing without straining other muscle groups.

"I brought you some homework, too," she informed him.

"Wonderful."

"There's a printed form for your human dynamics survey."

"Even more wonderful."

In order to kiss him, she got on her knees next to the bench. The first kisses were the little darters, rapid on his face and neck, like a bird feeding its young. Then she fastened onto his mouth to work her active tongue inside. As soon as she pulled away, she asked him, "Do you love me, Coley?"

"What?"

"I want you to tell me you love me."

It was a surprising request, but then Bree was nothing if she wasn't a source of the unexpected. "Yeah, I guess I do. Why?"

"I have to be sure, that's why." Her hand was inside his tank top, where she was exploring his pectorals and abdominals. "God, I love your muscles."

She swelled his ego like a pump. He was thoroughly aroused by this time. When he tried to sit up though, she pressed against his chest to keep him still. He could feel his voice going husky with breath: "You love a lot of stuff today, Bree. You love Oprah and you love my muscles."

"I love you, too. It wouldn't hurt you to say it."

Coley was about to say it, if for no other reason than to speed up the foreplay, when Bree noticed his Cindy Crawford poster. "Do you think I'm as attractive as she is?"

"Oh, sure."

"I mean, do you really think it though? Cindy Crawford is so beautiful, do you really think I am?"

"I said yes, right?" He ached for her. "They make these big stars look so good with makeup and lighting. In real life they wouldn't look so perfect." Maybe that would satisfy her.

It didn't. "But you might just be saying that. I don't want you just to say it."

"I'm not just saying it."

Bree ignored his denial. She was removing her blouse and bra, in a manner so rapid and nonchalant he was startled again. For a few seconds she let her eyes travel from the firm contours of her own flesh to the body of the supermodel. It seemed to Coley that she was attempting some sort of confirmation.

Then she locked her hands behind her neck and smiled at him. "You like?"

"Are you kiddin' me?" But when he started to sit up again, it was the same result: She pushed him down. "You love my body, but do you love me? If it was my picture on your ceiling instead of Cindy Crawford's, would that be just as good?"

"It wouldn't be just as good, it would be better." Coley pulled her head down so he could kiss her. It was a rough kiss, with a clashing of teeth.

"And you really mean that?"

"Yes, I really mean it. I don't have a condom, Bree."

"Why do we need one anyway?"

"I think we need one." As lathered as he was, it seemed miraculous that he retained some sliver of judgment.

But almost before these words of caution were out of his mouth, Bree said, "Look what I found." The packet she showed him was gold foil. She began to open it at the corner.

"Where did that come from?" Coley asked her.

"I don't know, I guess it's magic." She was giggling again in the dark but lyrical mix that somehow joined her unlikely blend of child and seductress. It was amazing the way she seemed to bring the same playful approach to sex as to the joy of miniature golf.

"Tell me you love me, Coley." She wasn't giggling now, or even smiling.

"Okay, okay, I do."

"No, but you have to *say* it. You've never told me you love me."

"Okay, I love you."

"And you really mean it?"

"Yeah, I mean it. I love you, Bree."

Chapter Nine

Sometimes he walked on his crutches, but at other times he used the cast as a walking cast. Bree carried his books for him even when he didn't need the help. She was as indulgent as a first-class flight attendant, at his side from class to class, helping him at his locker, up and down the stairs, and even after school when he needed his books carried to the parking lot. After a day or two, when he was confident on the supports, she nevertheless was still at his side.

She met Coley's parents for the first time the night they had the cookout. His father grilled steaks on the deck while Bree helped his mother chop the vegetables for a large tossed salad. Afterward he showed Bree the bull pen while his father made a few desultory passes on the tractor mower. He was taking a swipe at the taller grass on the far side of the lawn, near the fence.

"Does your father take care of all this landscaping?" Bree asked.

"Nope, he's just playing games with his newest fifteen-horsepower toy. My mother takes care of all this."

"It's so beautiful, she must work hard at it."

"She works too hard at it."

Coley demonstrated (as best he could) how you could gong the Reggie Jackson statue by hitting it in the right spot. By supporting his right side on a single crutch and lobbing a few balls in the direction of the statue, he tried to make his point about the location strategy that would have to be achieved.

"I don't get it," said Bree.

"I guess there's not much to get."

"Even the statue itself is, like, kind of weird. It doesn't belong with all the beautiful flowers and stuff."

"You sound just like my mother. Gonging the statue was just a hoot me 'n Patrick got going. He had the advantage, though, because he was right-handed. If he dropped down and threw sidearm, he could get right in under that elbow. He had a better angle."

"Who's Patrick?"

"He's my brother. He died four years ago."

"Oh, I'm sorry. I'm sorry I just blurted it out like that."

"It's okay. You didn't know, so why should you be sorry?"

"But I really am."

Coley's father approached to say, "You shouldn't be throwing."

"This isn't really throwing, we're just goofin' on the statue."

"I suggest you find some other form of goofing around, something that keeps you off your feet."

"Yeah, okay."

"This would be an easy way to hurt your arm or pull a muscle. Even worse, you might lose your balance and fall down."

"Well, we wouldn't want that, would we?"

"Don't be a smart-ass," said Ben. "If you need to impress Bree, find some other way of doing it."

Coley reddened angrily, but Bree began to giggle. "I don't need to look for ways to impress Bree," Coley said.

"I'm afraid he's right, Mr. Burke," Bree confirmed with a smile. "I'm already impressed."

"Don't let him snow you," said Dad to Bree. "He's not as good as he thinks he is."

Coley was pissed. He swung onto both crutches and headed for the deck. "What you mean is, I'm not as good as *you* think."

When he drove her home, Bree put her hand on the inside of his thigh, near his crotch. Coley gave a start; he could drive wearing the cast, but he didn't have his usual body control. "Take it easy, huh?"

She was biting at his earlobe, at times too hard for comfort. "Your dad says you need to goof off some way that keeps you off your feet."

"Yeah, that's what he says. We probably don't need to talk about him."

"I was just thinking of something you could do on your back, and it would be a lot of fun."

He didn't know how she could giggle and nibble and talk, all at the same time. "Not tonight, Bree, I have a headache."

"Very funny."

"There'll be other times," he said, turning one of her favorite phrases back on her.

"Very funny again. Are you going to disappoint me?" Her lower lip was extended, but in a mischievous way.

By the time he got home, it was after dark and his mother had just finished cleaning the grill with an S.O.S. pad. After she brewed herself a cup of Swiss mocha coffee, she plopped herself down on one of the deck chairs. Coley got a Mountain Dew from the fridge, then sat down beside her.

"I hope she had a good time," said his mother.

"Bree? Yeah, she had a good time. D'you like her?"

His mother didn't answer immediately, but it might have been just because she was sipping her coffee. "She's an easy girl to like, but I'd have to wonder if she's a happy person."

"She seemed like she was having a real good time. I'd say she was happy."

"I don't mean just tonight. What kind of life has she had?"

It should have been an easy question, but it wasn't. "I don't know a lot about her life before she moved here," Coley admitted.

"I would guess there's some unhappiness there."

"I would guess there's some unhappiness in everybody's life," he replied more defensively than he intended.

"True," she said. Her tone of voice was conciliatory.

"Sometimes she doesn't like talking about her private life." That was hedging the bet without a doubt, but he assumed his mother was right about troubling elements in Bree's past. He wished he knew what they were. He felt a little embarrassed because his own mother seemed to connect with her on a deeper level, after just one meeting, than he did.

"Anyway," she added, "I liked her and I think your father did too."

"I'm glad."

"I guess you must like her too, and that would be the real point, wouldn't it?"

It was dusk when he located Ruthie Roth's house along Wood Hill Road. The concrete slab that served as the front porch was somewhat askew. It needed to be jacked up, and it needed a railing of some sort to give it a finished look.

The neglected porch seemed to typify the nature of the neighborhood, which wasn't a slum exactly, but tacky enough. The unmowed yards were peppered with dandelions. Here and there was an overturned tricycle on the sidewalk. The house next to Ruthie's had shingle siding, but some of the sections were laid bare and covered over with roofing paper.

By the time Coley stepped clumsily from the car, Ruthie was already bouncing down the sidewalk. She jumped in the passenger's side. "This would be the Coley car," she declared.

"That's what it would be."

"It would have to be cool like this, or it couldn't qualify."

"Glad you like it," he said impatiently. *Will it have to be like this?* He started the engine before he asked her, "Where we goin'?"

"Let's go to the Coffee Barn."

The Coffee Barn was on the other side of the city, near the university. Coley grumbled, "That's way out in Campustown. There's got to be somethin' closer."

"That's where I want to go, dude. You want help with your homework, I get to choose the place. Quid pro quo."

Quid pro quo? Dude? Did Ruthie Roth practice annoying, or did it just come naturally? "Okay, okay," Coley agreed. "We'll go there if you really want to."

As soon as they pulled away from the curb, she lit up a cigarette. "You mind if I smoke?"

Coley wasn't sure. "What if I say yes?"

"It would be predictable if you said yes. Cigarette smoke would be just too toxic for the Coley car."

"Can you give that a rest, Ruthie?"

"I'll put the window down," she said. "I'll blow the smoke outside."

"You shouldn't smoke those anyway."

"That's what they say."

"Do you smoke those at home? Does your mother know?"

Before she answered, Ruthie thrust out her lower lip so as to exhale toward the visor. "My mother smokes about three packs a day while she parks herself in front of game shows and talk shows. She has never taken a hell of a lot of interest in much of anything I do."

Coley glanced in her direction while they waited at a red light.

Most of her face wasn't visible from this angle, though. At times it was hard not to feel sorry for her. This was one of those times.

He said, "Maybe you should count your blessings."

"Please, let's hear this."

"I was just thinkin' I might like it better if my parents were a little less interested in the things I do. Especially my old man. He even checks my fingernails sometimes because of the way it might affect my grip on the ball."

"Let's see your nails, then," said Ruthie.

Coley stuck his right hand in front of her face. "I don't pitch with this hand, but the left one's the same."

After she examined his fingers briefly, she said, "There's nothing to see here, they're not too long, not too short."

"That's the idea." Coley pulled his hand free and fastened it on the steering wheel. "That's my point."

"So you're bummed out because your parents aren't more indifferent. Is that what you're saying to me?"

"Yeah, that would be the word. Indifferent."

"So I'm supposed to, like, feel *sorry* for you because your parents don't ignore you quite enough?"

"Can you knock it off? I don't need anybody to feel sorry for me, I'm just pointin' out that there are two sides to everything. When it comes to conversation, that's probably the best I can do."

"Your daddy's rich and your ma is good-lookin'. Come to think of it, she's probably rich too; it's hard to find a successful real estate agent who isn't. You're the man-child with the golden arm. You can sign a contract for beaucoup bucks when you graduate. Am I slow to sympathize? Silly me."

Angry, Coley swerved the car to the curb and stopped. The heavy cast made the stop more sudden than he intended, but it didn't sideline his agenda. "Look, I really don't need this. What I could use is a little help with this one project, and even if it isn't all that important. You wanted me to pick you up at your house, which I did. You wanted to go to the Coffee Barn, and I agreed."

"Sorry."

"So back off or I'll take you back home. You can watch *Wheel of Fortune* with your mother."

"I'm trying to apologize. I don't know how to act."

"What do you mean, you don't know how to act?"

"I mean, I'm nervous." She threw her spent cigarette out the window with a snap.

Coley was cooled off enough to reenter the flow of traffic. "What's there to be nervous about? You're an actor. You're on the stage two or three times a year. That would make me nervous as hell."

"Think about it, for God's sake. This is you and this is me."

"Okay. I'm, like, thinkin' about it."

"Coley Burke and Ruthie Roth. Alone together. In your car. Can you just think about that?"

"Okay, okay." He followed the bend in MacArthur to avoid a Chevy Blazer that was straddling lanes. "Is that why you want to go to the Coffee Barn?"

"It's more adult. It's mostly college students. You can be different there, and they don't treat you with contempt. *Comprende?*"

"Yeah, I *comprende*. Let me ask you a question, Ruthie. In all the years I've known you did I ever make fun of you? Did I ever?"

"No, you've always just ignored me."

"Not always."

"Okay, not always. I stand corrected," Ruthie admitted.

"I'm sure there are lots of people I ignore—people I don't even know exist. I'm sure it's the same for you."

"Don't be defensive. The choice between being ridiculed and

being ignored is a no-brainer, if that's what you're hoping I'll say."

"I'm not hoping you'll say anything," Coley declared.

At the Coffee Barn they found a thick layer of cigarette haze, a glass counter housing a variety of pastries, a selection of four kinds of coffee, and very few empty tables. The first thing Ruthie said, surveying the setting, was, "What a dump."

"What did you say?"

"I said, 'What a dump.'" This time she said it with body language, a large hand resting on a large thrust hip.

"If that's the way you feel, why'd you want to come here?"

"I'm just practicing one of Martha's favorite lines from *Who's Afraid of Virginia Woolf?* In the play she says it all the time."

"Maybe you should be wearing the silver wig, just to take it to the next level. There's enough weirdos here you could do it and nobody would notice."

"Funny boy."

"Okay, so what d'you want? I'll buy; my mama's rich and my dad is good-lookin'."

Ruthie ordered some Turkish mocha coffee with whipped cream while Coley got a Coke. They found some space at a table more or less by themselves, although there were three other people nearby where tables were shoved together.

"So what are we working on?" Ruthie asked him.

"I'm supposed to make a values survey for human dynamics."

"What kind of a survey?"

"That's what I don't know. We're supposed to figure it out on our own."

"Well, you can't just go around asking people what they believe in, like Do you believe in God? What's your idea of love?"

"I know. That's why I need the help."

"Why are you even taking human dynamics?" she asked him.

"I need the grade. I've got a B and I need to keep it."

"You might as well take Dress for Success or some other crap like that."

"I couldn't fit it in my schedule. Look, I'm okay on my core courses, even Mrs. Alvarez says so."

Before she commented further, Ruthie took a sip of her coffee. "Why do you need a B in the course so bad?"

Coley was frustrated. "Because I'm gonna get a D in English, okay? If I'm lucky, that is. I need the grade point because it goes on a sliding scale according to your ACT scores. The NCAA makes the rules—they take away your scholarship if you don't have the right combination of grade point and ACT."

"Oh, God," she groaned. "Baseball. You're talking about your athletic scholarship."

Coley glanced uneasily at the people who occupied the other end of the table. One of them was a bearded guy wearing a tunic. It seemed like they were surrounded by intellectuals. This might be a place where Ruthie could feel at ease, but it wasn't the same for him. If he was going to sound like a dumb jock, the least they could do was keep it between themselves. He leaned closer in her direction before saying, "Can you, like, hold it down, okay?"

"I didn't realize I was being loud. Y'know, Coley, in some ways you're funny."

"How am I funny?"

"You're getting a D in English. I'm trying to think why that should happen."

"Don't talk like Mrs. Alvarez. If I wanted another lecture on not working up to my potential, I could just visit her office or talk to Grissom."

"I suppose you could. I'm just sitting here thinking that you're going to get a college scholarship for pitching baseball. Never mind

JAMES W. BENNETT

that you've got all the money in the world and you don't even need a scholarship. Never mind that you might not even graduate high school because of low grades in English."

"Don't go there, Ruthie, not now."

"I've got almost straight A's clear through high school," she continued, "and no money at all. I'll end up at the junior college and probably go into debt to do that. Who says life isn't fair?"

Coley stood up suddenly to leave. But he tripped on his cast and lost his balance. He fell heavily back into his chair. "I told you I don't need this shit."

"Okay, okay, I'm sorry. I promised to help you and I will."

She lit one of her cigarettes, during which time he managed to calm down. "I don't even know what to do the survey on," he admitted.

"Did Mrs. Alvarez give you any suggestions?"

"What's she got to do with it?"

"Well, I can't say for sure, but you just told me you were talking to her. What did the two of you talk about?"

"The usual, mostly. I'm an academic underachiever. I don't work up to my potential, yada, yada, yada." Then he thought for a moment before he said, "She brought up one weird thing, though."

"Which was?"

"She had a lot of information on my older brother."

"Patrick?"

"Yeah, Patrick. She said I might have some hidden guilt about his death. She said the guilt might have something to do with me coming up short on things I do."

"Even baseball?"

Coley was startled. "How did you know that?"

"I didn't, Coley," said Ruthie. "It was just a guess."

"Yeah, well. Anyway, it all seemed real weird and confusing. She even said some things about my mother."

"What things?"

"I told her how my mother is always dissin' Patrick. She puts him down."

"How does she put him down?"

"She always has to remind me how immature he was. And reckless. Thoughtless. Stuff like that."

Ruthie tried to blow a smoke ring. It didn't work; there was a ceiling fan moving too much air. She tried again before she said, "Maybe that's how your mother deals with guilt."

"Say what?" Coley was feeling more and more confused.

"I said—"

"I heard what you said," he interrupted, "but how does it make any sense? Patrick dies in a tragic accident, so she puts him down, and that's how she shows her guilt. Think about it."

"I *am* thinking about it." Ruthie was looking him straight in the eye. Even though the light wasn't bright, Coley noticed for the first time that she had green eyes. "Ruthie, your eyes are green."

She blew smoke in his face. "No, they're not. I have tiny red eyes."

"What the hell does that mean? No, don't tell me—somethin' else from the play."

"How'd you guess?"

"Never mind. Get back to the subject."

"Okay, what about this? Patrick was a hell-raiser. He got in trouble a lot. He was reckless—your word. Maybe when your mother puts him down, she's really trying to confess that she was a bad parent."

"A bad parent?"

"Yeah. What if she's afraid she didn't teach him enough discipline? What if she's afraid she wasn't strong enough to teach him values? He was a big superstar—who would care if he was an asshole from time to time?"

"That's where my dad would be at with it."

"Exactly. So what if your mother feels guilty because she let it get that way?"

Coley took a few minutes to reflect before he said, "What you're sayin' is, she's puttin' herself down when she disses him."

"More or less, yes."

"Ruthie, this is too much. This is not how I think."

"You can think this way if you give yourself a chance."

"Besides," he objected, "what does this have to do with a values survey?"

Ruthie was finishing her mocha by rasping off the bottom drops with the tip of her straw. "It could have everything to do with it. When there's a tragic death, how do people deal with their guilt?"

"Okay, but that's just a theory. This is supposed to be a survey."

"So, you've got a small start. Your own guilt. Your mother's."

"Which I don't even understand. Besides, that's only two."

"What about Mrs. Alvarez? What else did she say?"

His recollection came slowly but surely. Coley leaned all the way back in his chair and folded his arms across his chest. "She talked about it too," he finally said, quietly.

"Talked about what?"

"She talked about guilt. She talked about her husband. He died on a military training mission. She says she feels guilty about it even though she wasn't even there."

"Now we're up to three." She looked at her watch. "And we've only been discussing it for half an hour."

Coley was indeed seeing the light, but it was a light that seemed too bright and too vast. "Okay, what about you?" he asked Ruthie.

"What about me?" She stood up. "I think we should go now. I've got two chapters of trig waiting for me at home."

"Okay," said Coley, rising from his chair, "but what about your guilt? Your old man left you and your mother, right?"

"My 'old man,' as you put it, isn't dead. He's just an asshole."

"Okay, he's not dead. But he's still gone. Do you think you had somethin' to do with him takin' off?"

"I sure hope so." They were walking out the door.

While Coley pondered her response, Ruthie stopped long enough to thrust her hip again. "What a dump," she declared.

Chapter Ten

Bree went with him when he made his second visit to the sports medicine clinic.

Dr. Nugent was encouraging after he examined the new set of X rays. "This is about as good as we could have hoped for."

"Great. When can I pitch?"

The doctor smiled. "Not so fast. Let's talk about some rehabilitation first."

"Okay, I'm listening." As eager as Coley was, Dr. Nugent was all the way down the line by the book. Having removed the cast, he used his fingertips to probe the damaged ankle, which was white and stubbled like an old man who needed a shave. "Is there a whirlpool in the locker room at your high school?"

Coley grunted: "Yeah." Occasionally there were twinges of pain when the doctor pressed hard, but nothing acute. On the front of the ankle was a small greenish bruise about the size of a quarter. Bree was holding his arm when she wasn't gripping his hand. Coley wondered if Dr. Nugent thought it was weird, her being with him. *We must look like some lame and out-of-luck couple sucking up to a doctor for fertility drugs.*

Dr. Nugent gave him a plastic walking cast that was held in place by Velcro strips. "I want you to wear this when you're at school or walking in public places. Wear it anytime you're walking on an uneven surface, like your yard or a playing field."

"Can I throw?"

"Not yet. Until the time comes when you can really trust this ankle and drive on it, you'll probably overcompensate and strain other muscle groups."

"Come on."

"Like your arm, maybe. A pitcher with a sore ankle is one thing, but a pitcher with a bad arm is in trouble. You're listening to me, right?"

"Yeah, I am."

The doctor continued. "This is a manual of ankle exercises you can do at home. Follow the directions closely, don't improvise. Anytime you feel pain, it's time to stop and rest. You want to be aggressive enough so you push yourself right up to the threshold of pain, but don't go beyond that."

"Okay." Coley took the printed manual and folded it over so it could fit in his pocket. Bree took it from him, though, to put it in her purse.

"I'm going to send you out to the university so you can get an inflatable lace-up cast. You can run wearing it. Don't run on any uneven surface, though; run in the gym or on the track. Just remember, the rule of thumb is always the same: Push yourself to the point of pain and then back off."

"What about the stationary bike and stuff in the water?" Coley asked.

"Perfect. The more the better. You need to be in shape when you're ready to pitch."

On the drive home Coley enjoyed the freedom of the lighter, sleeker plastic cast. He was determined to follow all the rehab guidelines; thinking ahead, he realized he might be pitching again in two to three weeks, which would still be the month of May, which would still be before the start of the play-offs.

Bree squirmed close. "What did the doctor mean when he said you can't drive yet?"

JAMES W. BENNETT

"He wasn't talking about the car. He was talking about pitching. See, when you're pitching and using the right mechanics, you don't just step at the plate, you come down hard on your ankle and *drive* off it."

She sighed. "I guess I did ask, didn't I?"

Coley knew her patience would wear thin if he went into detail about pitching mechanics. He said, "You have no idea what it's like, Bree, to just blow a hitter away."

"I'm sure."

"You can't imagine what a rush it is. You just bring the heat and the batter is frozen in the box. He might as well have a piece of string in his hands instead of a bat, for all the good it's goin' to do him. He might as well be a statue; he might as well be *the* statue."

"I never heard you talk like this," she told him. "Can we change the subject?"

"Why?"

"It's, like, too exciting." Her hand was on his thigh, squeezing.

At first he thought she was teasing, but then he knew she wasn't. How talking about pitching would arouse her would have to be another Bree riddle. But it clearly did. He had to remind himself to watch the road.

"Let's pull over," she said. "You're getting me excited."

"I can't pull off here."

"At the rest stop, then," she urged.

"Didn't we already pass it?"

"Not yet."

It was only a mile to the rest stop, but to Coley it felt like an hour. When they exited and he swiftly skirted the parked semis, Bree pointed to a remote parking space beneath the shade of a mature elm tree.

Despite the presence of the clumsy cast and the awkwardness of the bucket seats, their lovemaking was swift and sure. The traffic that came and went intermittently was as inconsequential as the clouds.

The aftermath of this spontaneous afternoon delight, Coley decided, ought to be as good a time as any. "I've got a question," he told her.

"So what's the question?" She was dragging her fingernails along the side of his face.

"I want to know if you're a virgin."

"You want to know what?"

"You don't have to, like, be offended; it's just something I'm curious about."

"Why would you be curious about that? Anyway, isn't that an awful personal question?"

"Bree, we're at the point where we can be personal. We have an intimate relationship, which means we can discuss private things with each other."

"How can I be a virgin when we make love all the time?"

"That's not what I mean. Did you ever have sex with any other guy before we met?" He was thinking of Kershaw but not saying so.

"I just don't know why you'd ask me a question like that. It's pretty insulting, you know."

"A question like what?" he asked.

"You know what I mean. A question like, Are you a virgin?" She was sitting upright in her own seat. Fully dressed.

"I'm sorry if I insulted you. I didn't mean to. I'm only asking because I'm curious, like I said."

"I don't understand why you're curious about a thing like that. I don't know why you'd even ask me that."

"Now you're pissed." Confused, Coley started the car.

"Why shouldn't I be? We're making love together, which is the most intimate thing two people can do, and out of the blue you ask me if I'm a virgin." As if to emphasize the distance she was bent on establishing, she wrapped her seatbelt into place and locked it down.

It didn't take him long to get the car up to 75 mph. "How can you call it out of the blue? I mean it's, like, right when we're fucking, right after we're done, and I ask you a question about your sex life. That's not out of the blue. It would be out of the blue if I asked you, 'How did your math test come out?'"

"Please don't call it fucking," she said. "And wouldn't you be pissed?"

"Wouldn't I be pissed what?"

"If I asked you a question like that, wouldn't you be pissed?"

"No," Coley declared. "Ask me anything you want and I'll tell you. You can even ask me any question you want about Gloria."

"I don't want to talk about her. Why would I want to talk about *her*?"

"She's just an example. I was trying to make a point." He was annoyed this was going so badly. In a way he wished he'd never asked, but in another way he was convinced there was an important point to be made about intimacy in a relationship. Not that he could do a good job of making it, or even that she would want to get it.

"Of course I'm a virgin," she said quietly, staring straight through the windshield.

"We don't have to talk about it."

"I was a virgin until I met you. I'll never be one again, though, will I?"

"Okay, okay, we don't have to talk about it. I'm sorry I even brought it up." He wanted to believe her, but she wasn't convincing. By this point the whole question seemed utterly inconsequential. They finished the rest of the drive in silence.

It turned out that his rehab started with housework. He ran the vacuum cleaner, in his bare feet. Upstairs and down, shifting his weight firmly but carefully from one foot to the other, while leaning on the handle for security. Coley felt like it had to be a resourceful and clever strategy on his part, but it wasn't encouraging.

As long as he simply shifted his weight, he was fine, but if he attempted to lift his heel ever so slightly and get up on the ball of his foot, there was pain. He could put all his weight on his right side, but the moment he tried to twist his body or his leg even a trace, there was discomfort. Sometimes it was so acute it shocked him. There was just no place for torque. He was glum; this was a sprained ankle, for Christ's sake. Each time he was aware of the pain, he could feel an escalating level of anxiety in the pit of his stomach. It seemed like there was too much at stake and not enough time to deal with it.

His mother thought he had lost his mind. "I'm trying to remember the last time I saw you with one of those in your hand," she said. She was talking about the vacuum.

"Have your laughs."

"Are you okay?"

"I'm not losin' my mind, if that's what you mean."

"I think I meant your ankle," replied his mother.

He fudged the truth a bit by saying, "The ankle's doin' okay."

"If you're planning on taking care of the housework around here, maybe I should let Mrs. Trinh go?"

"Like I said, have your laughs."

Coley did his running in the gym while wearing the inflatable cast. The apparatus was clumsy, but it gave him confidence because it held the ankle completely rigid; it couldn't turn or roll. He got fatigued easily. He couldn't believe two or three weeks of inactivity could leave him out of shape, so he assumed he must be running with an unnatural gait by compensating for the cast. It didn't weigh much though.

It was stuffy in the gym. He took long drinks from the water fountain while he rested. Through the window next to the fountain he could see the guys practicing on the field. He chafed with impatience. The team's record was 6-3 (not counting the games in Florida). He longed to join them. Coach Mason told him he was welcome to be on the field and do what he could, but they both knew there wasn't any team activity that would improve his stamina or speed his recovery.

Some days, after he finished this private workout, he did join the squad on the field; he didn't participate in the team drills, but he sat on the bench. He passed the time, even during games, doing ankle lifts by means of a rope tied to a ten-pound weight that he looped over his toe.

At times he helped Jamie Quintero. Coley watched him throw and gave him pointers. At least it was a small contribution he could make.

Once, during a practice break, Rico asked him how the rehab was coming.

"It's coming good. I feel like I could do about anything I wanted."

"You have to be sure, though, man. Don't take any chances."

"Not you, too, Rico. That's what everybody tells me."

"Yeah, but it's true. I think I've got this thing figured out."

"What thing?"

"The scenario. Here's how it goes: We get you back at the end of the month for those two games in Peoria and Decatur. Assumin' we're still alive for the play-offs, that is, which I think we will be. If we're not, then we will be just as soon as you nail down those two."

"You're sayin' I should wait till the end of May before I pitch again."

"Here's what I'm sayin': It doesn't really matter how many games we win, as long as we get in the play-offs. That's startin' over, everybody is equal. That means we've got you on the mound, one hundred percent, and we're still in the play-offs. What could be better?"

"Is this Coach Mason's idea or yours?" Coley asked him.

"This is me, man. This is me talkin'. Mason might like the idea or he might not, I don't know."

"There's gonna be scouts, Rico. There's gonna be major-league scouts that wanna see me pitch, and the player draft is in June."

"You think I don't know that? You've already got a scholarship, though."

Coley made a face. "I know, but you're talkin' *college*. If I could get a decent contract, I'd rather sign."

"That's cool," Rico said. "I don't blame you. But just remember, the most scouts will show up for the play-offs."

"Yeah, that's true," Coley had to admit. Even when the advice sounded sensible, there was just too much of it.

Coach Mason joined them, and the conversation turned in the uncomfortable direction of academics. "How's the ankle?"

"Pretty good, I guess." What else could he say? "It'll be okay."

"How's your grades?"

"They'll be okay too."

"You're sure about that?"

"Yeah, they'll be okay. I've got Ruthie Roth helpin' me from time to time."

"Who's that?" the coach asked. "Never mind. Anybody that gets a progress report before the end of the month won't be eligible for the play-offs. You know that, don't you?"

"Hell, yes. How could I not know that? Coach, it's like I get this from my old man all the time, do I have to hear it from you, too?"

"I don't know. Do you?"

This pissed him off. Instead of answering, Coley reached for the walking cast. He hadn't come to practice so the coach could get on his case.

It almost blew Coley away when he discovered Bree was upset. She was pissed about the evening he spent with Ruthie Roth brainstorming on the human dynamics project. "Are you kiddin' me?"

"You're not supposed to date other girls," she said.

"This was no date. You know who Ruthie Roth is?"

"I've never heard of her."

"That's what I thought."

"That's not the point anyway. I've given myself to you, Coley, *all* of me."

It was the type of Bree remark that tended to knock him out of sync; nevertheless, he said, "If you knew who Ruthie was, you'd see how comical this is."

"I don't think there's anything funny. You're not supposed to date other girls."

"I told you this wasn't a date, are you listening to me? She helped me with a homework project. It was *homework*."

"Where did you do the homework?"

Coley sighed and shook his head. This was nuts. "We went to this place called the Coffee Barn. It's out in Campustown."

"I know where it is," Bree informed him. Her flashing eyes

stared straight into his own. He couldn't believe how intense she was when she got mad. "That's a long way out there," she added.

"A hell of a long way." At least they agreed on something.

"Did you take her in your car?"

"Well, we sure as hell couldn't walk. That's, like, about four miles, at least."

"You took her in your car to the Coffee Barn, but it wasn't a date?"

"I'm tellin' you. It was *homework*. Look, Bree, someday I'll introduce you to Ruthie and you'll know how this whole conversation is out of touch."

Bree ignored this appeal. "I don't know why you couldn't just study at her house, if all it was was homework."

"Because she wanted to go to the Coffee Barn, so we did. She likes the college atmosphere. Can we drop this now?"

"You had a study date."

Coley needed another deep breath. "Okay, me 'n Ruthie had a study date. Let's have it your way. Can we drop it now?"

"A study date is still a date."

He couldn't take any more of this. "Yeah, we had a date. I gave her a corsage first, then we went to the Coffee Barn. Afterward, we spent the night at the Holiday Inn."

"You think it's funny, but it's not. You don't know what it means to hurt."

"What's that about?"

"You don't know what it means to hurt. You don't know what it means to *need*." The change in Bree was so sudden, but it wasn't just in her voice. It was her eyes. They had shifted from the hard, shallow glitter of anger to the opaque liquid of deep pools.

"What are you sayin' to me?" Coley was knocked out of rhythm again. Sometimes conversations with Bree were like games of *Star Quest;* you just never knew which direction to look for the next spaceship attack.

"You've always been popular. You've always been a big star. What do you know about *needing?*"

The green eyes had been flashing a moment ago; now they were glistening. You could almost fall into them, like down a well. A moment ago he had felt like a prisoner beneath a hot light; now he felt like he needed to become a shelter. He said, "I have to get at least a B in the course. If I don't, I could lose my baseball scholarship."

"Please don't make me hear about that again, okay?"

"What else can I say? That's the reality of the situation, that's the whole reason behind needin' her help."

"I could help you with homework," she said. "I'm a good student."

"I know, but Ruthie is a straight-A student. She helped me with geometry when we were sophomores."

"I could help you," Bree repeated.

"Yeah, well, look at it this way. Ruthie's a senior. She's, like, in the top two or three in the class. She's a theater geek, so I can't get distracted."

"You'd be distracted with me." It was a question that didn't sound like one.

"What do you think?" Coley asked her. "With you and me it'd be about five minutes of homework, then two hours in the sack."

Bree smiled for the first time. "Please don't say 'in the sack.'"

"Okay, we'd be having sex. Is that better? Enough study time with you, and I'd lose my scholarship for sure."

"If it wasn't for the grade you need, you wouldn't see her at all, would you?"

"Hell, no," Coley replied quickly.

"And you really mean that?"

"You want me to say it again?" The admission brought him an unexpected measure of regret, even if it was mostly the truth. "Like I said, someday I'll introduce her to you. You'll see."

"I don't want you to. I don't want to meet her. Promise me you won't go out with her again."

Coley felt too whipped to quarrel with the *going out* terminology. "Okay," he said.

"But you have to promise, though," Bree insisted.

"Okay, I promise."

Chapter Eleven

The trainer was a girl named Shannon who was a senior at the university majoring in sports medicine. She taped his ankle so heavily it felt like an artificial limb. "How's that feel?" she asked him.

"Stiff as a board," Coley replied.

"Good."

He threw batting practice for the first time. It was awkward. He hadn't worked from the mound since the injury, and the rigid right ankle made his drive and follow-through tentative.

He didn't try to get people out. All he wanted from this outing was to throw strikes and to be as comfortable and fluid as possible. His flat pitches were in the strike zone, but without much velocity. His teammates delighted in driving Coley's pitches clear to the fence, and sometimes even over it. He didn't care. *The only thing is to throw strikes and feel comfortable.*

After twenty minutes or so the sharp pain in his back surprised him. It came, unfamiliar and sudden. He stood up slowly, put his hands on his hips, and told the coach he'd had enough.

Coach Mason followed him to the bench. "You okay, Coley?"

"I'm fine, Coach," he lied. "That's enough for the first time." He was slipping into his nylon windbreaker.

The coach left to press another batting practice pitcher into service, but when Coley started to sit down, the pain stitched him like a knitting needle. Halfway down he was paralyzed for a moment or two, unable to move at all. The sweat broke out on his forehead and along his upper lip. When it passed, he sat on the bench with his elbows on his knees and his chin in his hands. *I've never had back pain like this before.*

"Are you okay?" asked the female voice.

He looked up to see it was Shannon, the trainer. "I'm fine," he told her.

"Why'd you stop?"

"I've just had enough for the first time, that's all. Go worry about someone else."

"Okay, amigo."

Coley knew what the problem was—back spasms. By compensating for the ankle, he was throwing unnaturally and putting strain on the left side of his back, which could lead to shoulder damage. Nothing could undercut the career of a pitcher faster than a sore arm.

His palms were sweating even though it wasn't hot. The next time he threw, maybe he should try it without the tape. He would have to treat the ankle as if it were whole, instead of babying it so much. It was the only way he would be able to drive off of it with torque and then follow through.

The next day he played again, for the first time in competition. He felt pretty strong in warm-ups, so he approached the coach. "Put me in left, okay?"

"You want to play left? You feel up to it?"

"I'll be fine in left. Just let me play."

"If you tell me the ankle feels good enough, I'll believe you." Coach Mason was looking him straight in the eye. "This whole rehab thing is up to you. When you say you're ready, I'll trust you."

"The ankle doesn't hurt." That much was true. He knew, too, that any back pain would vanish in left field. "Just put me in the outfield, I'll be fine."

The team was woefully shorthanded because it was an ACT

Saturday; at least three of the juniors were sitting in Champaign for standardized testing, and two other players were injured. Ingram had a broken finger, and Bobby Lovell was out for the rest of the week with a sprained wrist.

"Did Shannon tape you up?"

"I'm taped," Coley replied. It was a warm day, but not warm enough to account for the sweat beading on his face.

"Okay," the coach said, "go for it."

Coley's service in the outfield was uneventful. Running gingerly, but with minimal pain, he tracked down two fly balls in the fourth and cut off a single down the line in the fifth.

Swimming in the pool seemed to be the best way to give the ankle range-of-motion expression. In the water he could rotate the ankle freely, without pain. It made him optimistic to discover he could walk on the floor of the pool or kick slowly from the side. Or even, although he wasn't a very good swimmer, plow through the water in his thrashing freestyle with unrestrained flipper kicks with both legs.

He went to the deep end and scuttled along the bottom, feeling the definition of the tiny tiles with his fingers. He didn't know what intrusion of gravity it might have been that kept him down there. He might have been at the bottom of the sea, like the huge fish that took it to the limit against Santiago, the old fisherman. And then he wondered what it was that caused him to think of books at a time like this.

Bree joined him once while wearing her skimpy new fuchsia bikini. She was a strong and efficient swimmer—she seemed to slice through the water like a sea nymph. Coley swam after her with all the speed he could muster, but he couldn't catch her. She giggled like bells at his futile efforts to swim her down.

They frolicked until they were breathless, then rested against the side of the pool in the shallow end. "This is the best part of my rehab," he tried to say to her, speaking between bouts of gasping for air.

"You mean it?"

"Yeah. It keeps me in shape. It's fun."

"You mean it's fun when I'm here."

"That's what I mean. And there's no pain in the ankle."

"Maybe I should come more often."

"Maybe." He had enough breath now to kiss her, so he did. She brought her tongue with the usual fervor. Coley peeled back the shoulder strap of her top to take a look at the dramatic ribbon of white her tan line made. He was aroused immediately. He couldn't remember ever getting a woodie in the swimming pool but realized it was about to happen. It couldn't be modest, either—not with the blue nylon Speedo suit he was wearing. He knew that other people might enter the pool area at any moment.

This dilemma, though—if it even was one—faded when he saw the bruise. It was blue green, about the size of his little finger. It reached from her collarbone upward toward the flare of her shoulder.

"What's this?"

"What does it look like?" she said.

"It looks like a bruise."

"Then I suppose it is one." She darkened suddenly, like a stormy sky. She turned her head away.

"So how'd you get it?"

"I don't know, how do people get bruises? How do you get yours?"

"Usually playing sports," Coley replied.

"That's how I got mine," she declared. "I got it in PE when we were playing field hockey."

JAMES W. BENNETT

"On your shoulder?" He supposed it was possible to get a shoulder bruise playing field hockey, but not likely. "How did it really happen?"

"I told you how it happened, weren't you listening?"

"Yeah, I was." He was using the back of his hand to wipe some of the water from his eyes. "But I think you're hiding something."

"I don't know why you have to ask so many questions." With that, Bree hoisted herself onto the edge of the pool, then walked briskly to the first row of bleachers. She picked up her towel and began to fluff her hair.

Coley waited a few moments before he followed after her. "We're supposed to be in love. That means we aren't afraid to talk about private stuff."

"Is that what it means?" Her head was down, and the towel draped around her shoulders. "Okay, then, if you think you have to know. He beats me."

Before he replied, Coley leaned back, his shoulder blades against the second row of bleachers and his hands locked behind his neck. "You mean your father, don't you?"

"I mean my *step*father. I mean Burns."

"Okay, stepfather." Coley felt a surge of sympathy for her, joined with the urge to be protective. "How does he hit you?"

"He hits me. What are you asking?"

"I mean, does he, like, hit you with his fist, or does he slap you?"

She sighed. Her head was still down. With the corners of the towel she was wiping at her eyes. Coley wondered if she was crying or if it was just water from the pool. "Usually he slaps me."

"Usually? For what?"

"If I break a rule or talk to him with a smart mouth. How many questions are you going to ask?"

"I don't know how else to find out. It's like pullin' teeth with you, Bree. If you loved me like you say you do, you wouldn't make it so hard to find out."

"I *do* love you, you know I do. It just scares me to talk about it."

He put his hand on her shoulder where the bruise was. "He didn't give you this one by hittin' you."

"He grabbed me and threw me on the couch when I smarted off to him."

"What did you say that was like smarting off?"

"I told him I was going to see you as often as I wanted and there was nothing he could do to stop me."

"Jesus Christ." Coley leaned forward and rested his elbows on his knees. "I oughta come over to your house and pin his gut against his backbone."

Bree lifted her face to look at him. In her eyes was authentic terror. "You can never do that, Coley. You can never. You have no idea how strong he is."

"That's rich. I'm supposed to be afraid of a chickenshit who slaps girls around?"

"But you just can't. You just had to know, so I told you. But you can't ever try to do anything about it, or you'll just make it worse."

"What about your mother?"

"She's afraid of him as much as I am."

"But I mean, does he hit her, too?"

"Sometimes he does."

Coley's frustration was roiling in his stomach like nasty indigestion. "Why the hell don't you just leave? You and your mother, I mean. Let him find somebody else to slap around."

"Oh, God, I don't know. My mother loves him."

"How can you love somebody if you're afraid of them?"

Bree got to her feet. Now there were tears rolling down her face. "I don't know. Now do you see why I don't want you asking so many questions?"

"No. Tell me."

"Because there's no end to it. The questions get harder and harder, and I don't know the answers. Then you ask me why I don't know the answers."

"It's only because I care about you."

"If you really care about me, you'll drop the whole thing, because it can't go anywhere except more trouble. More trouble for me, I mean." Now Bree was crying harder; she turned to leave. Coley rose to follow her, but when she entered the girls' locker room, he was stopped in his tracks.

He pitched two innings against Danville, but he wasn't effective. Even worse, he wasn't effective because he couldn't throw with comfort or confidence. At times, when he tried to drive off the right ankle with real thrust or leverage, he felt pain that shot clear up to his knee. The fear that the ankle was damaged beyond even Dr. Nugent's assessment—or might be if he didn't protect it—caused him to try to throw with his upper body.

He couldn't abandon his fear of reinjuring the ankle. The pain along the left side of his back surfaced after the fifth or sixth hitter. He was afraid of developing a sore left shoulder.

Coley walked two of the Danville hitters, and then two more got base hits. Not the scratchy kind of dribbler or chopper, but bona fide ropes into the outfield. Giving up line drives wasn't something he was accustomed to. It wasn't a hot day, but with sweat beading on his face, he paced around the mound tentatively and played with the resin bag. He scanned the sparse crowd for faces of men he didn't know, men who might be professional scouts.

When he was done with the two innings Coach Mason wanted him to finish, he sat on the bench with his head down. The coach couldn't know Coley's level of discouragement and apprehensiveness, but he had to have some clue at least. He said, "Not bad for the first time out, Coley."

It was a lie, of course, but such a lie that seemed to join them at the hip.

The following Monday was the senior class trip. Coley didn't expect megafun from it, but at least it got him away from the old man's nagging, Grissom's class, and any sense of apprehension about the ankle.

There were three water slides. About the third time down the highest slide they started tossing girls into the receiving pond at the bottom. Higher and higher.

There were plenty of squeals of delight and big-time yuks, but the lifeguards were blowing the whistle on it. Nobody paid any attention. Once, Coley launched Gloria so hard into the waiting basin that she nearly lost the top of her suit. When she came up for air, she flipped him off.

David Huff was the best at the game. He was a huge tackle on the football team who spent most of his spare time pumping iron. He already had a full ride to Notre Dame. He tossed Brooke Womack ten feet into the air the last time down. She made a mammoth splash when she smacked the water's surface. It was the final straw; the guards roped off the staircase and started identifying culprits. By the time they finished, Coley was kicked out, along with four others, including Kershaw and Huff.

Laughing madly, they made their way to the pool, where they stretched out in some vinyl loungers.

Coley turned to David Huff and asked, "Where'd you get the beer?"

"Brought it with." Huff was drinking his beer from a can, but the can was disguised by a wraparound Styrofoam Pepsi-Cola container. Bobby Lovell was using the same disguise.

"You got any more? I wouldn't mind havin' one today."

"In the bus, not here."

"Which bus?"

"Number three," Huff informed him. "There's a cooler under the third or fourth seat on the left side."

"You mind if I get one?"

"Go for it."

Coley made his way to the parking lot, where he found the bus and the cooler. There were four cans of Keystone left in gritty water swimming with puny ice cubes. The beer was cool, but not cold. He put the can in one of the soft-drink wraps before he headed back across the parking lot.

Now that he was alone and the ruckus was over, he found himself slipping into the brooding mode. He began scrolling the same issues that seemed to torment him every day: *What if I'm not eligible for the play-offs? Is it really true that Bree's stepfather beats her? But why would she lie about something like that? Is there anything actually wrong with my ankle or is it all in my head? You can have phantom pain from an injury. That's called psychosomatic, according to human dynamics class. Combat veterans even have phantom pains in limbs that have been amputated. It's the memory of it in their subconscious mind.*

He was hungry. He made his way through the crowd until he found the concession area. There were inside tables located beneath ceiling fans; a jukebox was playing old pop hits. Outside there was a small pond nearby, surrounded by a shady grove of picnic tables. Ruthie Roth was sitting there, by herself.

Coley approached her. "What's up, R.R.?"

"Are you lost? Your cool friends are over by the water slides and the pool."

"I got kicked out." He took a seat next to her on the bench.

"I heard."

Coley took a long pull on the beer. He wished it was colder. "Why are you by yourself?"

"I vant . . . to be . . . alone," she camped.

"Save it for the theater."

"What a dump!"

"You heard me," he said. "You won't have any fun all by yourself."

"Why do people like you have such a hard time understanding that being alone isn't a form of punishment? But if you have to know, I only came on the trip because I thought Mrs. Alvarez was going to be here. I thought she was one of the chaperones; I was wrong."

"You got a problem or something?"

"No, I don't have a problem." Her exasperation was evident. "Yes, I've got a problem. More than one. Who doesn't? That's not the point, though. I enjoy talking to her."

"You mean you like talkin' to her just for fun?"

"That's what I mean." Ruthie was staring straight at him. "Why is that such a stretch for you?"

"Don't start the smart-ass stuff, okay? Come on—I'll buy you some lunch."

"You're going to buy me lunch." It was a question.

"Sure," Coley replied. *This will probably make it a* date *in*

Bree's mind, he couldn't help thinking. "Why not? My cat is rich and my dog is good-lookin'."

"Funny, funny boy. There might actually be some hope for you yet."

Ruthie insisted on eating at one of the tables in the grove. "My skin can't stand much sun," she said.

Looking at the mottled, pale flesh of her arms, Coley assumed she was telling the truth. "A little sun would do you good," he said. "You put that theater makeup all over your skin, what's wrong with a little sun? At least the sun is natural."

"Theater makeup washes right off," she replied. "A sunburn doesn't."

"Okay, okay. What're you havin'?" he asked her.

"Okay, then. I'd like a plain hot dog and a Pepsi. Make that a Diet Pepsi."

For himself Coley bought three chili dogs and the Big Barrel Pepsi, the thirty-two ouncer. He got a lid from a cardboard box so he could carry all the food down the incline to the picnic table. He wolfed down one of the dogs before Ruthie had a chance to ask, "What are we going to talk about?"

"I need help with a book report for Grissom," he replied.

"So that's the catch."

"It's not a catch. If you don't want to talk about it, fine."

"You did that report on *The Old Man and the Sea.* What happened to that?"

"Grissom didn't like it. She says I missed all the symbolic stuff."

"Yeah?" Ruthie took a bite of her hot dog.

Coley had so much food in his mouth he had to jam it to the side in order to speak. "She's all bent out of shape on some symbols of Jesus Christ. She was all over my case. She wants me to reread the parts about the old fisherman carrying the mast from his boat up the hill to his house."

Ruthie wasn't very sympathetic. She wanted Coley to try to see it Mrs. Grissom's way.

"What is this 'her way' that you want me to see?"

"Hemingway is using symbolism. He means for old Santiago to be a Christ figure."

"What's that supposed to mean, 'a Christ figure'?" Coley demanded.

"It means Hemingway is using the old man as a symbol of Christ. The Passion, the Resurrection, the whole bit."

"I can see him guttin' it out. I can see courage. But not this other stuff."

"'This other stuff,' as you call it, is what makes literature," said Ruthie. She was being pleasant, but Coley had to wonder how soon she would run out of patience and break out the sarcasm. *This is what makes literature?* Coley finished the last of the beer before he began swilling down the Pepsi.

"Let's change the subject," he said.

"Okay, what's the new topic?"

"I need help with another book report."

"That's changing the subject?"

"Sort of, it is, yeah."

"Why don't you just do the revision like Grissom wants you to?"

"I can't get into that heavy stuff, I really can't," he said glumly. "I think it'd be easier to start over with another book."

Ruthie Roth sighed and took a long swallow of her Pepsi. "Okay," she said. "What kind of help this time?"

"Well, to start with, I need a book to report on."

"You want me to choose a book for you. After that, shall I just go ahead and read it for you and write your outline?"

"Don't start the sarcasm, Ruthie. I told you I've got a lot on my mind."

The conversation went in fits and starts because they were trying to talk with their mouths full. "What about that questionnaire for human dynamics we worked on?" she wanted to know.

"It's not done yet."

"It's not done yet?"

"I'm still workin' on it."

"How much have you finished?"

"Never mind that, I need a book to report on."

Before Ruthie continued, she finished her hot dog and washed it down with some of her soft drink. "Have you ever read *Mice and Men?*"

"*Mice and Men?* Didn't they make a movie of that?"

"*Of Mice and Men,* by John Steinbeck. Have you read it?"

"I don't think so."

"Okay, then, that's my recommendation."

"How long is it?" Coley wanted to know.

"It's very short. It's practically nothing more than a long short story."

"Because I need a book that's short with large print."

She was bobbing her head up and down before he'd finished the sentence. "I'm way ahead of you on this, you can trust me."

Coley was halfway done with the third chili dog. "So what's it about?"

"*Of Mice and Men?*"

"Are we talkin' about some other book here? Tell me what it's about."

"It's about a guy with brains and a guy with brawn. Come to think of it," said Ruthie, "it could be about you and me."

"I don't know what you're talkin' about."

"Me neither. It was just a thought."

For a few minutes Coley was silent. *Of Mice and Men* might have been one of the books Mrs. Alvarez had given him that day. "You better not be makin' fun of me."

"Why is that?" she asked.

"I'll take you over to the water slide and throw you down it."

She was laughing. "I didn't bring a bathing suit."

"That'll be your problem. I'll toss you big time."

"You wouldn't dare."

Coley had never seen her laugh this much before. He was glad she was enjoying herself, but he wasn't done with the questions quite yet. "Is it out on video?" he asked her.

"Is what on video?"

"*Of Mice and Men.* Can I get it at Blockbuster?"

"Oh, how would I know? Don't start with the dumbing down, it's not really you. If you want to watch it on video, at least you should read it first."

"Now you sound like Mrs. Alvarez," he declared.

"You could do worse."

Chapter Twelve

Supper was grilled hot dogs and hamburgers on the deck. Coley was throwing halfheartedly in the bull pen, testing the ankle. He never knew when there would be pain. Sometimes never, sometimes immediately. Sometimes only a minor, nagging twinge, but other times a pain so sharp it shocked him.

His father came to watch, cradling his third martini. He asked Coley if he was going to pitch against Jacksonville.

"I don't know. Coach wants me to."

"If he wants you to, why don't you know?"

"I just don't know, that's all." He grunted as he threw a good-velocity fastball that whistled under the elbow of Reggie Jackson's closed stance.

"Do you feel okay?" his father asked him.

"Yeah, I'm all right." It was the easiest answer, always the easiest.

"Then you need to pitch. You're not going to impress any major-league scouts if you're sitting on the bench and watching the game like some cheerleader."

"It's the ankle," said Coley, realizing how lame it sounded even as the words came out.

"What about the ankle?"

"I don't know. I can't trust it yet."

"You can't trust it. What the hell is that supposed to mean?"

"It means I never know when there will be pain. When I throw, I can't just cut it loose. I can only throw tentative."

"It won't work if you throw tentative."

"That's what I'm tryin' to say. I'm afraid I'll hurt my arm. Dr. Nugent said there's nothin' worse than a sore arm for a pitcher."

"Do we need Dr. Nugent to tell us this? It should be as plain as the nose on your face. Dr. Nugent also told you that there's absolutely nothing wrong with your ankle at this point. Even the last X rays show no damage whatsoever."

"X rays are one thing, but real life is another thing."

"Real life," his father repeated the words with contempt. He took a couple of swallows of the cocktail before he continued, "I'll tell you about real life. The fact is there's nothing wrong with your ankle. It's all in your head. You can see that, can't you?"

It had occurred to him more than once, which was the confusing part. "It might be," he said honestly. "It happens sometimes with rehab. Sometimes the mental part is harder to get over than the physical part."

"Don't lecture me about sports injuries and rehab!" Ben Burke sputtered. "Remember who you're talking to here—do you think there's anything about baseball you've thought of that I haven't?"

"Oh, hell no."

"Why don't we just put the cards on the table here, Coley? The thing standing in your way is your head, not your ankle."

"Maybe that's what I'm tryin' to tell you. Sometimes the physical part of an injury heals faster than the mental part. I won't be ready to pitch—not really *pitch*—until I have confidence in it."

"In your case that means the lack of mental toughness. It's always been your problem; you have all the talent in the world, but you lack the killer instinct."

"I've heard it all before, okay?" He lobbed a puny change-up toward the plate.

"This time it's the ankle. It's turning into an excuse to fail. You don't have an injury anymore, you *had* an injury."

Coley felt the confusion contracting his insides. The worst part was he was afraid his old man was right; at least he couldn't think of a way to dispute what he was saying. He vented his frustration by unleashing a pain-free, fearless 93 mph heater, which caught the statue right along the ribcage and sounded a fortissimo *gong* that reverberated through the neighborhood.

He tossed the glove to the ground and headed toward the house. "The next thing you'll be reminding me about is how tough Patrick was."

"You could do a lot worse. Patrick was a bulldog when it came to mental toughness. Why do you think he was on a major-league roster by age twenty?"

Coley continued toward the house, and his father followed a few paces behind. "I'm not Patrick," said Coley.

His father ignored the remark and replied, "You can find any hiding place you want, but I'm asking you why you might not pitch on Monday and you haven't got an answer."

"You can get off my case any time. Maybe I want to win. What if I told you I want us to win the state?"

"Somebody has to win the state, it might as well be you. What's the point?"

"The point is," Coley replied as he eased back into one of the vinyl strap loungers on the deck, "if I'm one hundred percent, we have a better chance of winnin' the play-offs. If I'm only fifty percent, we're just like most of the other teams."

But Ben Burke was shaking his head aggressively even as he found his way into a nearby deck chair. "No, no, no. This isn't about winning high school play-off games. It's about your future."

Coley's mother brought some tossed salad to the table and said,

"Maybe we can shelve this argument now. It's almost time to eat."
She returned to the kitchen to fetch plates and silverware.

"You probably think I don't know you batted right-handed
down in Florida," said Ben.

Coley's surprise lasted scarcely a millisecond. "I doubted if it
would get past you," he replied.

"I suppose that was for God and country too, huh? Stupid. It
was stupid."

"The guys want to win. They're winnin' without me, most of
the time. They don't need me to get past the regionals. But if I'm
one hundred percent for the sectionals and the state, we could go
all the way."

"Tell me whose idea this is."

"It's mine. It's Rico's. It's Coach Mason's. The guys want to
win. I want to win."

There was a pitcher of premixed martinis on the table. Ben
Burke freshened his drink before he said, "Major-league scouts
don't give a damn who wins or loses high school play-off games.
Nobody does."

"*We* do. *We* give a damn."

"Don't interrupt. Five years from now nobody will even
remember who was in the play-offs or who won. But five years
from now your future may be carved out. That has to be your priority, not who wins the regional tournament."

His mother returned to set plates on the table. "I thought I
told you it was time to put this argument to rest. I'd like to have
a pleasant supper together, if that's possible." She began forking
wieners into buns. Coley could see the muscles of her jaw
working.

"I'm just trying to explain something to him about his future,"
said his father.

"I know," said Mom. "I've been listening, in spite of my best intentions."

"Then maybe you could help out here."

"I doubt it. I don't think you'd want to hear what I think. Hot dog or hamburger?" she asked him.

"Jesus Christ! Do you think we could cut to the chase here?"

That's when Coley knew the old man was getting drunk: When his mother sent out these kinds of warning signals, you'd better pay attention, unless you wanted the shit to hit the fan. His dad knew it as well as he did.

"Ketchup and mustard?"

"Tell him to think about his future first. That's all I'm askin' here—is that so hard?"

"Let me ask you something," she said to Ben. Before she asked, she took a seat and began tonging tomato wedges onto her bed of chopped iceberg. "Isn't playing on a team supposed to teach you to subordinate your own individual needs to the good of the group?"

"That's a different subject."

"Yes, I suppose it is. It seems to be Coley's subject. He seems to be saying he feels bonded to his teammates. He's concerned about their success as well as his own."

"If this is all you've got to contribute, why don't you just drop out of the discussion?"

"I warned you, didn't I?" His mother's eyes were flashing. "I told you to leave me out of this altogether, but you chose not to listen. Your son wants to share in the team experience, but you can't see any value in it."

As rapidly as he could, Coley prepared himself three hot dogs and squeezed on the ketchup and mustard. If this was going to be a knock-down-drag-out, he wasn't sure he could stand to be in the vicinity.

"The hell with the *team experience*! If he can get his head together, this kid may be standing at the threshold of a major-league career! Is that so hard to grasp?"

Coley scrambled for a cold Pepsi.

"The difference between the two boys," she said, "is right in front of your face. What you usually refer to as 'lack of a killer instinct' is actually a decent human being."

"It's chickenshit," argued Ben. "It's the excuse to fail."

"It's called *character*," countered his mother. "If Patrick had had any of it, he'd probably still be alive today."

Coley stood up. "Y'all can knock this off right now, or I'm leavin'."

"You better leave," said his father quietly through clenched teeth.

Coley went downstairs with his food. He could hear the shrill tenor of their raised voices through the open windows. He couldn't make out all the words, but he knew them anyway.

You can't live your dreams of glory through your sons, his mother would say. *They weren't put here to fulfill your fantasies.*

They were put here to fulfill something! Dad would reply. *Some level of greatness, some measure of achievement. If it was up to you, all they'd need to do is keep the yard mowed and go to S.A.D.D. meetings after school!*

And his mother would answer by saying in a shrill voice, *Maybe you'd better think of another example! If Patrick had ever shown any interest in S.A.D.D. meetings, he'd probably still be alive today!*

How dare you say that to me? Patrick died in a boating accident! How dare you blame me for his death? Drunk, he would sputter out his indignation in a chain of incoherent protestations.

While his mother, more adept than he in the war-of-words format, and certainly far more composed, would ever so slightly turn the knife that she had skillfully inserted: *Did I say that? Did you hear me blame you for Patrick's death?*

The words might change—some of them, at least—but the agenda itself wouldn't change, and neither would the animosity. Coley turned up his TV loud to blot out the fevered pitch of their angry voices. He gobbled all three hot dogs in less than two minutes washing them down aggressively with Pepsi-Cola.

He heard the front door slam hard enough to shake it from its hinges. His father, drunk and pitiful, would swim his way to the Buick in the driveway.

He heard the car door slam. He heard the tires squeal on the asphalt. He knew his father was headed straight for the country club, where he would find his way to the bar and spend the rest of the evening in the company of some good-old-boy drinking buddies.

The day she told him she was pregnant they were swimming in the pool. His ankle felt great, even when he swam at full speed in pursuit of her.

Giggling breathlessly while hanging on to the side, she said to him, "I've got big news. You're going to be a daddy."

The demeanor didn't fit the message. She might have been telling him she'd just scored some floor tickets for a concert. "What's that supposed to mean?"

"Just what I said. I'm pregnant."

"You can't be pregnant. How do you know?"

"Why can't I be? I took a home pregnancy test." But she wasn't giggling anymore.

"Bullshit, you can't be sure."

"I'm completely sure. I just told you, I took a home pregnancy test."

"But we used a rubber most of the time."

"Most of the time, we did," she replied. Bree lifted herself so she was seated on the edge of the pool.

"That's what I said. We use a rubber almost all the time."

"*Almost,* Coley, but not *all* the time. It only takes once."

"Don't tell me what it takes! Let's say you're right; you don't even seem bothered about it."

"Well I am bothered about it, but it's not the end of the world."

" 'It's not the end of the world?' That's all you've got to say about it? 'It's not the end of the world?' "

"What else should I say?" Bree asked. "You want me to go out and hang myself or something?" She stood up and walked away without waiting for an answer.

Jesus Christ, Coley thought. He could feel a knot of apprehension contracting his stomach. He swung himself out of the pool in order to follow her.

Bree was on the first row of bleachers, toweling her face and hair. "I thought you might be a little bit pleased," she said between the folds.

"Pleased? You're knocked up and I should be happy about it? Are you crazy?"

"Don't say 'knocked up.' I'm going to have a baby; *your* baby. I was hoping that at least a part of you would be happy about it."

"What part would that be, Bree? The part that wants to spend my life driving a cab or working at the 7-Eleven?"

"I should have known you'd be totally negative about this."

Coley sighed deeply three or four times before using his own towel to dry his face. It was bad enough to get a girl pregnant, but if she didn't even seem to have much regret about it . . . where would you go with a thing like that?

"You say you're sure?"

"That's what I said."

"When was your last period?" he wanted to know.

"I'm two weeks late," she replied.

"Two weeks? That doesn't prove anything," he said.

"I already told you about the home pregnancy test. Didn't I tell you about the Clear Blue Easy?"

That must be the name of the product, he thought. "So how does it work, anyway?"

"It takes a sample of your urine, and if two blue lines appear, it means you're pregnant. It has ninety-nine percent accuracy, right on the package."

"So where does it get this urine sample? Do you have to pee in a bottle or something?"

"Why are you being like this?"

"Being like what? I'm asking you how the test works. I'm just tryin' to get some facts here."

Near the shallow end of the pool four girls approached the apron, giggling and pushing one another. Bree was watching them.

"Hey. Did you hear me?"

"I heard you, I heard you. You don't go in a cup or anything, you just let your pee dribble on this applicator while you're going to the toilet. Are you satisfied now, Coley? This is, like, real embarrassing."

"What's embarrassing is what the hell we're going to do about it if you're pregnant."

"I don't know what you mean—'*do* about it'? If I'm pregnant, I'm pregnant."

This remark would have signaled extra trouble if he had allowed himself to pursue it. Instead he asked her, "What's an applicator?"

"It sticks out from the main part of the test—it's about the size of a Popsicle stick."

"You piss on a Popsicle stick and that can tell you if you're pregnant? You can't go by something like that, Bree, you have to go to a clinic like Planned Parenthood or something."

"Don't tell me what I have to do!" She turned her flashing eyes to glare at him.

"I'm just sayin' you can't be sure that way."

"There are two tests in the package. I can do the test over again in a couple of days. Does that satisfy you?" She was on her feet now, wrapping the towel around her waist.

"No way am I satisfied, not with Clear Blue Easy or any other test you do at home. There's no way to be sure unless you go to a clinic or a doctor's office."

"So why is that so important? Why is it so important to be sure? Time will take care of it, and then there won't be any doubt at all."

Coley couldn't believe the words coming out of her mouth. "Why is it so important to be sure?"

"Yes. Why is it?"

"Because if you're pregnant, we have to get an abortion."

"*We* have to get an abortion?"

"Okay, you. We have to start makin' plans, because you can't get one unless you go to Chicago or St. Louis."

"I would never get an abortion." It wasn't a defiant statement, but a simple declaration, the way he'd heard her once decline the purchase of a fish sandwich at McDonald's.

"You would never get an abortion." Coley could only repeat her own words back to her while he felt his contracted stomach sinking like a stone.

"I could never get one." Her back was to him now; she was heading toward the girls' locker room. He heard her say, "That's the same thing as killing a baby."

"Killing babies? Do you have any idea what you're sayin' here?" He was too stunned to chase after her. Besides, she was already rounding the cinder-block partition that hid the entrance to the girls' lockers. Their voices must have been louder than he'd realized—the four girls in the shallow end had stopped talking to look and listen.

Coley didn't get much sleep the next two nights, but he pitched against MacArthur on Saturday. For three innings he had his best stuff. He felt loose and strong and fearless, with respect to the ankle. It was a very warm day, which gave him a comfort zone of sweat. He struck out three hitters on called strikes and three others swinging.

In the fourth inning he saw his mother's Century 21 car pull up behind the left-field bleachers. Bree was with her. Just after he retired the first MacArthur hitter on a pop-up, he could see that Bree and his mother had taken seats in the bleachers next to his father. Bree said something that made his mother laugh.

On the next pitch Coley had pain. First in the ankle, then a few pitches later in the lower back again, the sharp, slicing kind that told him he was pitching with his upper body. How could he truly dwell on pitching mechanics though? After he walked a batter, the next two made outs; but the outs were both solid line drives to the left fielder. Line-drive outs were worse than cheap hits.

As soon as Coley got to the bench, he slumped his head and draped a towel over it. "Take me out," he said to the coach. "That's enough."

"That's all you want?" asked the surprised Mason.

"That's enough. I went four innings."

"You looked strong, Coley. You feel okay?"

"I'm good," he lied. "I just need to pace myself."

"Okay, you're the boss."

Coley bent over to wrap a towel around the ankle, but it was a hollow gesture. There was nothing the matter with his ankle or any other part of his anatomy. It was abundantly clear to him now that any problems he might have that affected his pitching were strictly mental. *It's all in my head. All of it.*

He spent the rest of the game with his head bowed down and his elbows on his knees. He wore the towel over his head like a cowl. Rico and Jamie persisted in trying to comfort him.

"We're still gonna win, man," said Quintero.

"I know," Coley murmured. He didn't lift the towel, though.

"We're still good," Rico reminded him. "Don't forget the whole scenario. We're not even into the regionals yet."

"I know." During the last two innings he glanced at the crowd once or twice from beneath the hem of the towel. His father was gone, but his mother was still there and so was Bree. *She's pregnant,* he thought to himself. *She's knocked up and she doesn't want to do anything about it. Her stepfather beats her up. Jesus Christ.*

A seldom-used sub named Robert Greene was walking batters, thus prolonging the game. At this moment Coley couldn't imagine how he might have cared any less. A hard knot was constricted in his stomach; the world was closing in somehow. *Oh shit,* was all he could think.

JAMES W. BENNETT

Chapter Thirteen

Coley avoided Bree for the next week, although it wasn't easy. He only knew he needed the space. He could only think of the child—his child—growing inside of her. *Was that real?*

She was persistent on the phone, but he let the answering machine take her calls. He didn't return them. If his mother wrote down the messages, he didn't return those, either. Thank God Bree didn't have her own car or she would have been parked on his doorstep.

At school they had none of the same classes, but they did have the same study hall, fourth hour. He got passes from Coach so he could spend the period shooting baskets in the gym, or he got passes from Mrs. Alvarez so he could go to the computer lab. He even changed his hall routes during passing periods so he wouldn't have to confront her between classes. All of this purposeful maneuvering, though, was so stressful it convinced him that you couldn't really make much *space* for yourself if you had to work so hard to manufacture it.

They went to an invitational tournament in Galesburg, which took them out of town for three days. Coley's sense of relief was strong, and it showed on the mound. He pitched the first four innings against Moline, during which time he was overpowering. He struck out six, walked one, and gave up only two hits. The hits were both cheap flares; nobody made solid contact against him.

Two days later, on Sunday, he pitched the last three innings against Galesburg. The team was behind 4-3 when he took the mound, but Galesburg never got a sniff of another run. Or even a hit, for that matter. Coley was as strong as he'd ever been—maybe even stronger. He struck out seven batters while retiring the other two on infield pop-ups.

He pitched with no pain at all, driving fearlessly on an ankle that felt whole again. Before he pitched to the final batter, he stood on the mound in a euphoric condition that bordered on ecstasy. The weather was perfect, the maple trees were rich with the leaves of May. In the bluest sky were a few puffy white clouds that seemed pasted in a permanent position.

His father was not among the spectators, lurking to challenge him to move his game "to the next level" or give him a sermon about mental toughness. Bree wasn't watching him, to remind him of his paternity dilemma. There was no answering machine back at the motel, and he was throwing 94 mph fastballs without effort or pain. He had his best velocity and his best control. As disproportionate as it seemed for a pitcher who had thrown five no-hitters by the end of his junior year, he felt so free there were actually tears forming in his eyes.

And they were winning. He felt like part of a unit that could beat anybody.

On the bus ride home Coach Mason sat beside him for a while. "Only ten days till the regional," said the coach.

"I know," Coley replied.

"If you're gonna have that kind of stuff, we won't have to stop at that level; we'll be set for the play-offs all the way to state."

Did the coach want a promise? "I'm ready," said Coley. "I'm all the way back. Just give me the ball."

"Did you have any pain at all out there?"

"None. I was all the way loose. I was free. Too bad there weren't any scouts watchin'."

JAMES W. BENNETT

"There was, though. I saw Bobby Ricci in the third row behind the plate. Had the JUGS gun and his clipboard."

"Who's Bobby Ricci, Coach?"

"He scouts for the Royals. I used to watch him pitch at Comiskey Park."

"I never heard of him."

"You're young, that's why. You kids never heard of anybody. If I asked you who Robin Roberts was, you probably couldn't tell me."

"Who's Robin Roberts?"

"Exactly."

The coach was making his rounds on the bus, encouraging, scolding, advising. When he left to talk to Jamie Quintero, Rico moved in next to Coley.

"We're just about where we want to be, man," Rico said. "You were awesome up here."

Coley smiled. "I felt good."

"You trust me now? I told you I had the scenario. Two weeks till regionals; we're gonna be zoned."

"Ten days," Coley corrected.

"Ten days, two weeks, what's the difference; we're there, dude."

Coley knew he was right. A state championship wasn't out of the question.

Rico changed the subject. "I got an offer," he said.

"What offer?"

"I got a letter from Wabash Valley. They offered me a scholie."

"That's great, Rico. Didn't I tell you to be patient?"

"Yeah, but it's still only JC. Can they do that?"

"Can they do what?"

"Can they give full rides? Can a junior college do that?"

"Sure, if they're Division One. Wabash Valley is Division One.

I think they can give up to eight or ten scholarships, somethin'
like that."

"You think it's for real, then."

"Sure it's for real," Coley replied.

"But it's still only junior college," his friend persisted.

"A full ride is a full ride, though. Plus there's guys that get pro
contracts out of JCs. It happens all the time." Coley could see his
friend felt better. He added, "And don't forget, this is only your
first offer. Keep patient like I told you. There'll be others."

"You think so?"

"I've been right so far, haven't I?" The two of them sat in
silence for a few miles. Some of the guys were sleeping. The corn in
the fields that zoomed by was ankle-high. Coley knew he had to tell
someone about it, and it might as well be Rico.

He told him about Bree's pregnancy.

"Are you sure? Is she sure?"

"That's what she says. She took one of those home pregnancy
tests."

"It could be wrong, though."

"I know, I know." But Coley could feel his stomach tighten. "I
could, like, hope, but she seems real sure about it."

"Didn't you use a rubber, man?"

"Most of the time we did."

"Most of the time?"

"Yeah, Rico, that's what I said. *Most* of the time. A few times
we just got carried away." Coley spoke louder than he meant to.
He glanced around to make sure nobody was eavesdropping.

"What are you gonna do?" Rico finally asked him.

"I don't know. She says she won't have an abortion."

"Say what?"

At this moment words just came as if by rote; Coley felt like he was talking to himself. "She says she won't have an abortion. She calls it baby killing."

"Jesus Christ."

"That's what I say."

Rico had a hold on Coley's arm. "Look, Coley," he said. Coley had never seen Rico's face so earnest. "Just don't do anything stupid."

"I think I already did."

"Okay, but you know what I'm talkin' about. The play-offs are close. We can go all the way."

"Don't you think I know that?"

"I'm just sayin'."

"I know what you're sayin'. I want to win a championship as much as anybody else; you know that."

"That's why I'm sayin' just be cool. We sure as hell won't win one without you."

"Okay, okay, what more d'you want me to say?" He was almost sorry he'd brought the subject up at all.

You couldn't deliberately avoid Bree for several days running, like Coley had done, and not pay the price. The good news was, when they went to the prom, enough time had elapsed for her fury to diminish. The bad news was that he pitched another shaky game in the meantime, so that the glory of his Galesburg performance was reduced to a fading memory.

Before he left the house on prom night, Coley took a moment to check his appearance in the full-length mirror in the living room. But only because his mother insisted, just after telling him how nice he looked. The tux *was* a perfect fit, and the ruffled shirt had a certain preposterous elegance. She helped him pin his boutonniere into place on his lapel.

She insisted on taking his picture, despite his protestations. His dad was still on the golf course, so he didn't have to endure a series of family snaps as well.

He was out the door, even had his car keys out, when she called after him, "You're forgetting something, huh?"

It was the corsage. His mother handed him the white box from the florist, but she asked, "Are you okay?"

"I'm fine, why?"

"I don't know. Is there something bothering you?"

"No, I'm fine," he lied. "There's nothin' wrong."

At Bree's house the tension was excruciating. First of all was the drawn-out session of picture taking. The cocksure, aggressive stepfather had the two of them posing in front of the fireplace mantel, in front of Grandma's handed-down antique wing chair, and even on the front porch next to the rose trellis. Group pictures, too. In each instance when he gave directions of where to stand or even *how* to stand, the two women, Bree and her mother, fluttered into place like obedient children in a holiday pageant.

When it was Bree's mother's turn to work the camera, she seemed shaky and uncertain. Their fear of this self-important man, their need to please him, was something Coley had noticed before, but never had it seemed so vivid. And he didn't have to wonder, throughout the ordeal of photographing, if he hit them, but only how, and how often, and how hard. Bree's dress was a stunning, formfitting off-the-shoulder sheath of royal blue silk, and the body that she poured into it was that of a woman. But she followed her stepfather's every direction promptly, like a little girl.

When it was time for them to leave, Burns got deep into Coley's space on the front porch. It seemed like his face was no more than a foot away. "We want Bree home by one A.M.," he said evenly. "We don't believe in this after-prom nonsense."

"That's fine with me," Coley replied. Instead of stepping back, though, to create distance, he moved slightly forward an inch or two so he was nearly chest-to-chest.

"This after-prom crap is usually just an excuse for backseat hanky-panky. You and I know that, don't we?" There was a hint of a smile at the corners of his mouth but no humor associated with it.

Coley stood up straight so he could gain what felt like an advantage; he stared directly into the flat gray eyes. Coley was nearly two inches taller, but the two of them probably weighed about the same. It was confrontational body language for sure, but Coley couldn't seem to help himself. He knew the time would come, but the knowledge seemed to calm him. "I said that's fine with me."

"You can't talk to him like that," was the first thing Bree said to him when they got in the car. "What d'you think you're doing?"

"He can kiss my ass."

"But you got right in his face, Coley. You can't do that."

"Right. I should be scared of him."

"It won't be you he'll take it out on. Can't you understand that?" She was adjusting the elastic under her arms that held the dress up. Not much of her legs was concealed by the dress in the careless way she sat.

"He doesn't scare me," Coley repeated. "If he wants to try me one time, I'll be ready."

"I keep telling you it won't be you, it'll be me. And my mom. I don't want to talk about it anymore. We have to change the subject."

The prom was held at Laurel Country Club. In the spacious atrium there was a reception area with tables of hors d'oeuvres, desserts, and six different versions of nonalcoholic blends in large punch bowls. A string orchestra of old men in black tuxedos was playing background music on a small stage. A large banner with words made out of stars glued together proclaimed the theme of the prom: A NIGHT TO REMEMBER.

It was crowded, so they took their cups of punch to the terrace. A heavy wrought-iron balustrade was anchored to the flagstone floor. It was after dark, so the last golfers were already in the clubhouse. The dense trees on the golf course were only visible as silhouettes. Bree told him she was still pregnant.

"What does that mean, *still* pregnant'?" Coley asked. "Did you think it would go away like a sore throat or something?"

"Please don't be sarcastic. I mean I took the home pregnancy test again."

"I told you what I think of your home pregnancy test."

"I bet you don't know anything about it. Anyway, the result was the same; you're going to be a father."

"Would you stop sayin' that?"

"Even if I do, it won't change the fact. Aren't you excited at all, Coley?"

"Excited? Give me a break. I'm not ready to be anybody's father. I can't even deal with my own. Or yours."

"Burns is not my father."

"Stepfather, then. Why the hell would you want to be a mother? You can get an abortion in St. Louis or Chicago. It's a legal operation and safe. And I'll pay for it."

"I told you before, I can't think about an abortion." She turned her back.

"This is not just your decision, for Christ's sake, it's both of us. If there's a baby, it's *ours,* not just yours." He shook his head; already he was exasperated, and the prom had just begun. A Night to Remember. Oh, yeah.

JAMES W. BENNETT

With her back still turned, Bree began slowly walking away. "And I don't want to talk about it anymore." Her words bounced with an improbable gaiety. "This is the prom, so we can't spend the whole time arguing."

"*I* want to talk about it," Coley demanded. He followed her down the steps on the terrace.

They were headed toward the tee by the fourth green. It was too dark to walk fast or carelessly. "All you want is to talk about an abortion," she said.

When he caught up, he took her hand. "It's not just that, Bree. It's our future. We have to talk about our future."

"Baseball, that's what you mean. Your future as a superstar."

"That's part of it, but not all. Maybe pro baseball, maybe college, maybe who knows? You've got two years of high school left."

"I wouldn't be the only teenage mother going to school."

"For Christ's sake, would you listen to yourself?" He took her by the shoulders and turned her so he could look into her eyes. "Bree. This is important. You can't just ride off into the sunset with a thing like this. There are consequences."

She stared straight back at him. "Maybe you should have thought about consequences when you were getting what you wanted. You wanted all of me, and I gave it to you, remember?"

"You want to try that again? I wanted sex with you, and you, like, just put up with it. Is that it?"

She turned away again. He followed her to the wooden gazebo next to the tee. They sat on one of the benches, in the dark; the only light was that which the moon provided.

"If you take me to California, I'll get an abortion," Bree told him with no prelude or warning.

"I thought abortion was baby killing. What happened to that?"

"I've decided a relationship means giving as well as taking," she replied simply. "You can't have everything the way you want it."

"Take you to California? What's that about?"

"It's far away from here. It's far away from Burns. And they have lots of baseball teams there; you told me so yourself."

"They don't have rookie leagues in California," he explained to her. "The Gulf Coast League is in Florida."

"Florida's where I grew up. I hope you remember, I told you that. But if we go to Florida, we can't be anywhere close to West Palm Beach. That's where my real dad lives."

As always, he found himself off balance. He didn't know which of these agendas to address first. "What are you tryin' to say?"

"If we go to Florida, you can pitch. You told me that's where the big-league teams are."

"The Gulf Coast League," Coley muttered. "That's a rookie league."

"Is it close to West Palm Beach?"

"It's all the way on the other side of the state. The other coast."

"Okay, then, the Gulf Coast League. You can pitch there for a while till you're ready to move up to the major leagues. We can get married and be on our own."

"I can't sign with any team until after the major-league player draft," he explained, "and that's almost a month away. And where does getting married come from? You're not even old enough to get married without your parents' consent."

"Okay, the married part's not important. That could come later. But we could be together and on our own. Maybe you can get abortions in Florida without your parents' consent."

"Jesus Christ, you've been thinkin' about this. You've got a *plan*."

"Of course I've been thinking about it," Bree replied promptly. "Who wouldn't? The problem's not going to go away on its own."

"What you're really lookin' for is a way to get away from your stepfather."

"Okay, so? Is that such a crime? But that's not all of it, Coley, I'm in love with you. I'm carrying your baby."

Coley slumped. She was exhausting at times. As preposterous as her Florida plan was, he almost had to admire its thoroughness. "What about school?" he asked. He aimed the question at his forearms, which were resting on his knees. The carnation boutonniere was tweaking his nostrils. "You've still got two years of high school left."

"Every state has high schools," was the answer.

Coley stood up. "I have to take a leak," he announced. It was twenty yards or so to the clump of evergreens where there was more than enough privacy to relieve himself. But his head swam with alternatives and unresolved dilemmas. If they went to Fort Myers, he could throw for major-league scouts and she could get an abortion. Nobody would know about the procedure—not his parents, not her parents. But it was nuts, with the play-offs coming up and graduation. He could be arrested for kidnapping because she wasn't even sixteen yet. For that matter, what would living with Bree be like, except maybe hopping up and down on blazing AstroTurf? It was all too overwhelming. You started to think crazy when you were cornered.

When he got back to the gazebo, he asked her, "What about your real father?"

"What about him?"

"You said he's in West Palm Beach."

"That's why we can't go there," Bree replied. "If we go to Florida, it can't be there."

"Why not? Maybe he can help you."

"Help me?"

"Okay, help *us*. Is that better?"

"I don't know how he could help anyone. He's the reason I had to move to Illinois and live with Burns." She stood up and walked away before she said, "Now you're going to start asking me questions again."

"You're the one who wants to elope and run off to Florida. Maybe I have the right to check out some alternatives."

"But you're asking me all those questions again."

Coley had to ignore her resistance. "How did he force you to live with your mom and Burns?" He was speaking to her back across the twelve feet of gazebo floor.

"He didn't force it, he *caused* it. And I told you I don't want to talk about it. We should change the subject."

"We don't have to change the subject. I'm askin' you *how* did he cause it?"

There was a long pause before she said clearly, "Okay, if you just have to know, I'll tell you. He assaulted me."

"He did what?"

"I said, he assaulted me."

"I heard what you said, but what's it supposed to mean?" Coley got to his feet. His eyes were adjusted to the dark, so he could see that her shoulders were shaking. She was crying. He went across and folded her up in his arms from behind. Her shoulders were cold. He took off his tux jacket in order to wrap it around her shoulders. Her cheeks were wet with tears.

She sobbed so long and so hard that when she tried to speak, he shushed her. Her sorrow seemed to come from some desperate and wretched private chamber. Observing the intensity of it, Coley couldn't help but think of what his mother had once said, that there must be some real unhappiness in Bree's background. "It's okay," he told her. "You don't have to talk."

When she turned around so they were face-to-face, she gathered the jacket tighter around her shoulders. She was still crying, but it was only tears now, no more convulsions. Her face was on his chest. He felt so large and she felt so small. "It was sex," said Bree. "In family court they call it assault. Sexual assault."

"Oh, Jesus."

"It's okay, Coley, I can tell you."

"What did he do to you?"

"He did everything."

"Everything? You mean he even . . ." Coley wanted the right words.

"I mean everything." Bree took care of the words. "Even penetration."

"Penetration."

"That's the word they use for it in family court. Penetration. He raped me."

"More than once?"

"A lot more than once. Sometimes he even took videos of us doing it."

"Jesus."

"Stop saying that, huh?"

"But why did you let him, Bree? Why didn't you stop him?"

"I was only in the seventh and eighth grades. What was I supposed to do?"

"What does he do now?" Coley asked her.

"He doesn't do anything, except go to the racetrack or hang out in bars. He's on some kind of disability."

"Why did you stay, Bree? Why didn't you leave?"

"I was in junior high, where was I going to go?" The tears were still running down her cheeks in steady streams, but her voice was firm, if flat. "My mom had left to go live with Burns, not that I blame her. My real dad lives in these cheap hotels that you rent by the month."

"Why isn't he in jail? If you rape your own daughter, you should be in jail, for Christ's sake."

"The court took me out of his house and gave my mother custody. But he got off with a suspended sentence because of his disability. He had a lawyer who got him off because of some loophole having to do with his medication."

"Okay, okay, you don't have to talk about it anymore."

"I'm glad I told you, but you have to tell me you love me. You have to say it, Coley."

Coley couldn't find a reason not to say it. "Okay, Bree, I love you."

"And you have to mean it."

"Okay, I mean it." He took the clean, starched handkerchief from his pocket and began dabbing gently at the tears on her face. "We don't have to talk about it anymore," he repeated. He found himself subdued by her desperately shocking, evil story. *She left a father who raped her so she could live with one who slaps her around.* For once he didn't doubt that she was telling the truth, which made it all the more sobering.

Not that it changed anything, he reminded himself with a sigh. She was still pregnant and he didn't know what to do. Elope to Florida? Coley could hear the music from the orchestra across the way. He almost forgot, they were at the prom, right? And there was laughter. The pond carried sound across the still night air like a stereo.

Her tears dried, Bree was using the handkerchief to blow her nose. She was better now, she said. Coley searched for something to tell her but couldn't find the words. He finally said, "Hey, Bree. This is a night to remember, huh?"

JAMES W. BENNETT

"I don't know how you can be sarcastic at a time like this."

"Sooner or later we have to lighten this up. You wanna dance?"

"Dance?"

"We might as well. It's the *prom.*"

"Okay," she said, handing over the wadded-up handkerchief. "Let's."

Chapter Fourteen

Coley pitched a perfect game at Morton on Wednesday. At least, it would have been a perfect game if the rains hadn't come in the fifth inning. Pitching without pain or fear, he struck out twelve of the fifteen batters he faced. He wondered how.

On the bus ride home his soaked teammates were jubilant and raucous. All the talk was about the play-offs and a shot at the state championship. Coley longed to share their euphoria, but the Bree factor created a gulf between him and the others.

"We're totally grooved now," said Jamie Quintero. "No reason we can't go all the way."

"There's always luck involved," said Coley. "Any time you're in a single-elimination tournament, you've always got the luck factor."

"Nah. We're grooved. We're in the zone. In a play-off schedule we can have you on the mound practically every time out."

Rico was tweaking him. He pulled Coley's cap down to cover his eyes. "Too bad you don't get credit for a perfect game."

Coley couldn't help laughing. "Who cares?" he asked into the dark.

Rico spanked the bill of the cap. "No perfect game unless you go the full seven. You'll always have the asterik on this one."

"That's *asterisk* to you, dim," Coley replied. He pulled himself free from the binding cap.

The next morning he used his free period to browse the newspapers in the library. On page 3 of the sports section the *Journal-Star* had a three-column action photo of Coley at the instant of his release point. He looked at the picture for several moments. *What do people see?* he wondered. *Other people?*

The caption beneath the picture said, A MAN AMONG BOYS. Coley didn't know whether to laugh or cry. The only time he felt like a man was when he was with Bree, but it never lasted.

He sensed her before he saw her. Mrs. Alvarez was reading over his shoulder.

"What's it like?" she asked him.

"What's what like?"

"What's it like to be a sports hero?" She took the chair beside him.

"That's what I keep tryin' to figure out," said Coley honestly. "What're you doin' here?"

"I work here," Mrs. Alvarez replied quietly. "I'm allowed to visit the library."

"Funny." It didn't allay his sense of alarm. "But you want to see me, don't you?"

"Yes. I need to talk to you. But I want you to come to my office. The library isn't very private."

After Coley put the newspaper back, he followed Mrs. Alvarez down the hall, but with a sense of doom.

She didn't beat around the bush. As soon as they both got seated, she said, "There's not an easy way for me to say this, Coley. Mrs. Grissom has turned in another progress report on you."

"Not another one. It would mean I'm not eligible."

"I'm afraid that's true. There's not an easy way to say that, either."

"But I turned in an extra book report."

"I wouldn't know about that," said Mrs. Alvarez, "but here's the statement." She pushed the green form across her desk so Coley could examine it. The "Unsatisfactory Progress" box was checked with a bold *X,* and at the bottom was Mrs. Grissom's signature.

He pushed the form back to her before he murmured, "Oh, Jesus. She's just nailing me because I don't get all the symbolism she sees."

Mrs. Alvarez said, "I'm really sorry. I know how much the play-offs mean to you."

He slumped in his chair and closed his eyes. "Mrs. Alvarez, why were you asking me about being a sports star?"

"You mean in the library?"

"That's what I mean. It seems like a cruel joke, but that wouldn't be like you."

"No, Coley, I would never make a cruel joke with you. It was an honest question. I wonder what big success is like. The kind that gets a person lots of exposure."

"But why? Why are you askin' me a thing like that? At a time like this?"

"Because I think you're afraid of it. Success, I mean."

Coley thought, *What's that supposed to mean?*

"Success can be scary," she went on. "Sometimes it can be scarier than failure."

"Are you talking about baseball?"

"Baseball, relationships, academic success. All of it. I think succeeding is scary to you."

"Next thing, you'll be sounding like my old man: Looking for excuses to fail. Becoming a coward."

"What if your *father* is right in some respects?"

"In some respects?" Coley felt the anger rising along his neck. "In *what* respects?!"

She paused before she answered. "Please don't raise your voice. You don't need to. I know how hard it must be for you to talk

JAMES W. BENNETT

about these issues, particularly at this moment. But maybe this is the best moment. Or the only one."

Coley bit his tongue. "In what respects," he said, tersely but quietly.

"What if your father wants to do the right thing, but for the wrong reason?"

"This is about Patrick, isn't it?"

"It *is* about Patrick. Your academic slide coincided with his death. We talked about this once before—about the guilt associated with the death of young people. Your mother deals with it, your father deals with it, and you deal with it. Even when you don't realize it."

"And that's why I'm afraid to succeed, even in baseball."

"Please don't oversimplify. The things that go on in your family are linked to the tragic death of your older brother, in my opinion. I have to keep stressing that—it's only my opinion."

"The next thing, you'll be suggesting that all three of us go somewhere for family counseling."

"I can think of worse ideas," the counselor replied quietly. "But for right now I'd just like you to think about it. Not today, not tomorrow, when you're so terribly disappointed. But sometime."

Coley didn't reply. He felt numb. "I can't talk about this now."

"I know."

For several moments he simply stared at the green form on the desk. "There's no way I can make this up, is there?" It wasn't really a question, though.

"Not this semester."

"This semester? Mrs. Alvarez, this semester is all there is. I'm a senior." The sense of desperation that was sinking in was overwhelming. *God, wait till the old man hears about this.*

"I wish there were something I could do," the counselor said, her sincerity plain. Then she repeated herself by saying, "I really am sorry."

He dragged himself to his locker, for no reason other than to avoid people who might want to talk. On the shelf at the top was his copy of *The Old Man and the Sea,* in plain view. *The Old Man and Me* would be more like it. He slammed the door shut so hard he rattled all the lockers in the vicinity. *Wait till the old man hears about this.*

He sat by himself in his car at lunchtime and munched on a few Fritos; he didn't have much appetite. If he went to the cafeteria, he would see Rico and his other teammates. What could he say to *them*?

He walked like a zombie from class to class after lunch, choosing passing routes in the hallways that would allow him to avoid any friends or teammates. And he sure as hell didn't want to make any contact with Bree.

After school he went quickly to his car. He could see his teammates on the baseball field beyond the parking lot, warming up and goofing off. He stood staring. He didn't—couldn't—move. There was no reason to join them now, not if he wasn't eligible. He wondered if he should tell the coach. But not now, no way.

He wouldn't be part of the fun. He wouldn't be part of the push to the play-offs. It humbled him to think how he was letting them all down.

Still dazed, he got behind the wheel. Snippets of his conversation with Mrs. Alvarez echoed in his head. Grissom's progress report was the last straw, but only the last one. He felt like he didn't know himself at all anymore. But he also felt like he wanted to.

On some level he was choosing. Ankle injuries, back spasms, a pregnant girlfriend, academic failure, confrontations at home, and whatever. He wanted to see himself as a victim, but it was getting harder all the time.

Could it be so simple as his father's claim that he lacked a killer instinct, which amounted to the same thing as needing a reason to fail? Was he opting for means to fail because he was afraid that success would be a dishonor to his dead brother? Were these notions as preposterous as they seemed?

He stared into the low sun for perhaps a full minute or more, still numb, until the players on the field were just silhouettes and his head ached.

He wondered where Bree was. Now he wanted to see her. She usually waited for him near the practice field or by his car. Not today. He went back inside the school, but she wasn't in the library or the cafeteria. He decided to cruise the streets that might track her direction home, in case she might be walking.

He drove along Jefferson Street and then Eleventh without seeing her, but on Monroe he spotted her walking by herself while hugging some books to her chest. She was moving so slowly it was more of a stroll than actual walking. He rolled down the passenger's window to call to her. "Get in the car, I'll give you a ride."

"Not now, Coley, I need to be alone."

"Will you get in the car, Bree?"

"Why aren't you at practice?" she wanted to know. But when she spoke, she didn't look in his direction.

"That's a story. If you get in, I'll tell you about it."

"Didn't you hear me? I said I need to be alone."

Coley was getting annoyed, crawling the car along the curb while trying to talk to her through the other window. "I can't do this forever, Bree. Come get in."

She moved into the passenger's seat demurely, while looking straight ahead. Her hair was loose, so it covered most of her face.

She was wearing her sunglasses. "Okay, so I'm here. But just don't start asking me lots of questions."

He headed the car toward Washington Park. "I got another progress report from Grissom," he told her quietly. "I'm ineligible."

"Oh, no."

"Believe it. That's why I'm not at practice. I'm not eligible."

"But why?"

"How do I know? You'd have to ask Grissom. I don't know what the bitch wants from me, anyway. Could you at least look at me? Would that be too much to ask?"

She didn't, though. She kept her eyes straight ahead. "I tried to tell you I'm not good company."

"I can't pitch again. I'm not eligible." He lifted her chin so he could look at her face.

"You better stop the car," she told him.

He stopped the car. When he removed her sunglasses, he could see that the left side of her face was swollen. Not grotesque or disfigured, but smoothed out so that there was no definition on that side, as if lacking a cheekbone. A blue green bruise was at the corner of the eye.

Bree wrenched her face away and replaced the sunglasses. "Are you satisfied now?" she asked. Her gaze was fixed out the windshield once again.

"Why did he do this?" Coley asked. "Why did he hit you?"

"We were late from prom."

"We were fifteen minutes late. He hit you for that?"

"It doesn't matter how long. We were late."

The intensity of his frustration was suddenly accelerated to a level he couldn't tolerate. He pounded the steering wheel with the heel of his hand before he said, "Jesus *Christ*!"

Chapter Fifteen

Flight 106 left O'Hare International Airport at 6:00 P.M. and landed in Orlando just after 9:30, Eastern time. Bree slept soundly on board, but Coley tossed and turned. He had taken some Dramamine just before takeoff, which made him drowsy, but not enough to put him under. He twisted uncomfortably in his cramped aisle 9 seat while the leading players in the dreams that troubled him came forward like the accusatory ghosts that tormented Ebenezer Scrooge on Christmas Eve. His mother. Mrs. Alvarez. Bree's mother. Mrs. Grissom. There may have been others, but in his disturbed awake-and-asleep condition he struggled to get rid of these tormentors. "Go away," he groaned at one point. "Leave me alone."

At Orlando International he stood dumbly in line at the Hertz rental counter. Bree was bouncy. "This is real close to Disney World," she said. "We could stay all night and spend the day there tomorrow."

"Yeah, really."

"It would be fun."

"It might be fun, but it wouldn't get us where we need to go."

"Oh, poop. Is this the way you're going to be?"

"Probably." When it was Coley's turn, he used his Visa card to pay for the Ford Escort. He said, "Miami," when the counter clerk asked for the drop-off point, and he rented the car for a full week. He'd also used the credit card to pay for the airline tickets and to get some cash. He had twelve hundred dollars in his pocket.

When they were putting their luggage, what there was of it, into the trunk of the car, Bree asked him why he'd said Miami. "We're going to the other coast, right?"

Coley sighed before he answered. "The same reason we flew to Orlando instead of directly to Fort Myers. Since I used the credit card, we'll be easy to track."

"Oh."

"The rest of the time we use cash. Anyone who wants to follow us will go to Orlando and then Miami."

"You really are smart, Coley. You really are."

"Oh, yeah. That's why I'm here with you and not going to graduate and trying to arrange a tryout for myself plus an abortion for you."

He was behind the wheel, and she was clinging to his arm with both hands. "Now, we're not going to have that kind of talk, okay? You'll just ruin everything if you only see the bad parts. We're free now."

"Yeah, that's sure how it feels."

They spent the night in a cheap motel near Lake Buena Vista called the Seaview. It was an ironic name for the place, since there wasn't any ocean for at least a hundred miles. What there was instead was a lot of truck traffic all through the night along Highway 4, which made sleeping difficult.

But not for Bree. She awoke early the next morning rested and refreshed. As soon as she got out of the shower, she was ready for action. She crawled on top of him so they could make love. But even as she was astride and he was thrusting, he couldn't help visualizing Bree in this position a few years earlier as a pleasure machine for a pathetic middle-aged groper.

The mental picture passed when he reached his climax, followed by the first moments of serenity he'd known in the past forty-eight hours. She curled up beside him and started to tweak his few chest hairs (as she often did) to annoy him. "You feel better now, don't you?" she purred.

"You know what, Bree, sex isn't the answer to everything."

"But you do feel better, so admit it." Saying this, she gave a firmer yank on one of the hairs.

"Ow! Knock it off!"

She pulled another one, stinging him sharply. "Not until you admit you feel a lot better."

"I feel a lot better." He found himself giggling.

"We're on our own, Coley. It's just the two of us now, with nobody to tell us what to do. We're in love and we're on our own."

He repeated her words, somewhat mellowed in spite of himself: "We're in love and we're on our own." Coley stared up at the four-bladed fan suspended from the ceiling, turning slowly and making a *click-click-clicking* noise as it wobbled on its uneven axis. It was hypnotic. *Numb is a lot better than stressed,* he couldn't help thinking. "I feel a lot better," he said in a monotone.

They stopped for breakfast at a McDonald's on the outskirts of a town named, appropriately enough, Baseball City. Bree was as buoyed and effervescent as she might have been winning the lottery or being chosen prom queen. Her appetite reflected her mood. She ate pancakes and sausage and hash browns, then ordered a cheese danish to top it off. She weighed only about 110 pounds, so Coley had to wonder where she was putting it all.

While she went to the bathroom, Coley took the opportunity to visit the pay phone next to the parking lot. He made it a point to have plenty of coins on hand, so he had enough to make the call home. While he heard the phone ringing, he could feel the knot swelling in his chest. Finally there was an answer: "You've reached the Burkes, but no one is able to answer the phone at this time. When you hear the tone, please leave your message." Coley heard the tone. Actually, he felt a measure of relief in speaking to the machine.

"Okay, Mother, this is Coley," he started out. After pausing, he continued, "We're okay, so you don't need to worry. Nobody's hurt or anything. I can't tell you where we are right now, but I will real soon. . . . I wish I could explain exactly what's going on, but I don't think I can. . . ." He paused to moisten his lips and swallow. He knew that the machine would not record a message longer than sixty seconds. "This all has to do with Bree and the fact her stepfather beats her. I had to get her away to a safer place. . . . It also has to do with me goin' ineligible for the play-offs, but I'm sure you know all about that by now. We'll get this all figured out sometime soon, and I'm sorry to put you through this. But I don't want you to worry."

Then he hung up. Leaving the message made him feel a little better, but he could only hope it would have the same effect on his mother.

Bree was waiting in the car when he slid behind the wheel. "Were you calling one of the Gulf Coast League teams?"

"No. I called my mother."

Bree sat up very straight in her seat at the same time she seemed to go pale. "What did she say?"

He started the car. "Nothing. She wasn't home. I left a message on the answering machine."

"You didn't tell her where we are?"

"No. I just told her not to worry. We can drop the subject now."

It took almost four hours to drive down to Fort Myers, owing in part to the fact that Coley took Highway 17. This was a road that meant passing through lots of towns and traffic signals, but he figured there would be fewer state patrol cars this way. He was right, but he still tensed up each time he spotted one.

They didn't get back on the interstate until just past the town of Cleveland. And even when they entered Fort Myers proper, Coley continued on to the south by way of Highway 865 all the way to Fort Myers Beach on Estero Island. The afternoon sun sparkled on the blue gulf waters just beyond the cocoa palms that flanked the roadway.

"It's so beautiful," said Bree.

Even though he was tired, Coley had to agree. It looked like paradise.

"So, so beautiful," she continued, "but why'd we go all the way through the city? I thought Fort Myers was where you'll get your tryout."

"I'll *ask* for a tryout," he corrected her. "Nothing's for certain. I just thought if we were out of town, we'd be harder to trace."

"You think of everything, Coley. Sometimes I'm amazed how smart you are."

"Oh, absolutely. I flunked English, I knocked you up, I'm not going to graduate high school—"

"Okay, you can just stop talking that way. I'm not going to let you ruin everything."

"I'm on the run, I could probably go to jail for kidnapping, I'm practically a genius, Bree."

"I said you can just stop. I'm not going to listen to that kind of talk."

They found a room in a motel called the Coral Cliffs, which was nice enough, if not elegant. There was nothing that looked like a cliff, but Coley assumed there were plenty of coral reefs offshore.

He parked the car in a rear corner of the parking lot, where some low-slung bougainvillea created partial shelter. Most of the vehicles in this spot wouldn't be visible from the road. He registered under the name of Mr. and Mrs. George Lenny by combining the two main characters from *Of Mice and Men*. Bree waited in the car while he completed the paperwork.

On the west side of the motel was a small swimming pool and a concrete patio adjacent to a modest tiki bar surrounded by plenty of recliners. The view of the ocean was breathtaking, all the way to Sanibel Island.

"Why did you get a reservation for only two nights?" Bree asked him.

"We can add more nights on if we want to."

"But it's just gorgeous here. I want to stay here longer."

"Maybe we will. But we can't live in a motel, Bree, nobody has enough money to do that. Sooner or later we'll have to find the kind of place where people live, like an apartment."

"But we can take care of all of that later, Coley."

After supper they sipped Pepsis and watched the sun go down on the water. There were quite a few other people nearby, mostly old folks. Latin music was playing on a karaoke near the bar, but not loud. Coley found it was hard to feel stressed in this ultra-mellow setting, or guilty, even though he had the inclination. "I've been to Sanibel Island," he told her.

"You have? When?"

"When I was little. My parents took me and my brother there on vacation."

"Can we go over there?" Bree asked eagerly. "Let's go out there tomorrow."

"Not tomorrow. We have stuff to get done."

"What stuff?"

"I have to go over to Lee County Stadium. That's where the Royals have their Gulf Coast offices."

"I don't know why you care about the Kansas City Royals. Who ever heard of them? Why don't you sign up with the Yankees or the Braves?"

"You don't just sign up, Bree, there's a major-league player draft in June. A team picks you, and you can sign with that team or you can go on with school and enter the next year's draft."

"Okay, so why the Kansas City Royals?"

"Because I'm hopin' to throw for Bobby Ricci. He saw me pitch at Galesburg on a day when I had my good stuff. Besides, he's a guy who's never contacted me or my old man. Nobody knows I even know who he is."

"Wow. You've really thought this through, huh, Coley?"

"Yes and no. Just don't tell me how smart I am."

Bree was wearing the turquoise bikini. Prone on her vinyl lounger and sipping on her long straw, she seemed at utter peace with the world. The sea breeze tossed her fine hair while the low sun highlighted its red value. She looked beautiful. "I still want to go to the island," she declared.

"We'll go after the abortion, how's that? We'll spend the day over there just beachcombing, swimming, maybe even a little scuba diving. How would you like that?"

"How am I supposed to get the abortion?"

"You can call the Fort Myers Planned Parenthood. We'll get their number out of the phone book in our room."

"What if they don't have one?"

"Then you can call the one in Cape Coral. It's just as close."

"But you'll have the car. You'll be gone for your tryout."

"I keep telling you it's not exactly the same thing as a tryout. Anyway, I won't be gone the whole day, just a couple of hours."

She flipped the hair out of her eyes before she answered. "Okay, I'll call."

"You'll call and make an appointment. I'll go to the baseball complex, you'll take care of the clinic arrangements. You said, 'What stuff,' well, that's the stuff."

"Okay, okay, I said I would. Now, we can't have any arguments, because it's too beautiful here."

Before they went to bed, Bree spent more time in the bathroom than she usually did, and the closed door represented unusual modesty. She slid in next to him beneath the sheets and kissed him, but didn't seem inclined to activate any foreplay. Coley didn't mind; in fact, it was almost a relief. He used the remote to switch off the TV.

There was plenty of available parking space in the Lee County Stadium complex. Besides the baseball stadium itself there was a network of offices in a sprawling, undistinguished one-story brick building. The building was a bit confusing in its orientation because the Twins and Red Sox also had offices there.

Coley was too early. A secretary in the Royals' wing told him that Bobby Ricci was in town, but he never arrived at the office before 10 A.M. She also told him that Ricci was more than just a scout, he was head of player development for the whole Kansas City organization.

This had to be a good omen. Ricci was not only in town, but he was a honcho. Coley could feel his nervousness easing a bit. He killed some time by wandering around the stadium, where maintenance crews were doing some small-scale remodeling and painting. Mostly on the concession stands. There were individual chair seats in the sections near home plate, but the rest was just bleachers, extending along both foul lines. It was a nice stadium, but Coley had played in better ones—Pete Vonachen Stadium in Peoria, for example, and Jack Horenberger Field at Illinois Wesleyan University. He decided not to go back to Ricci's office until at least ten thirty. It wouldn't look too good if the man hadn't had a little time to make some phone calls or check his mail.

When he did go back, he was received immediately, which was a good feeling. The tight spot in his stomach loosened a little. "Come in, come in," said Ricci. "I saw you pitch not so long ago." They shook hands as Coley entered the office. It was a small room with a nice desk. The framed photographs on the wall were so numerous he couldn't help but think of Patrick's old room, back at home.

Ricci was a small, wiry man with thinning black hair. His deep tan suggested that when he wasn't at a baseball field watching players, he was probably on the golf course. He also seemed to have a penchant for saying things twice. "Have a seat, have a seat." Coley sat down.

"Do you drink coffee? I don't have much else I can offer you."

"No, no coffee. No, thanks."

"What was that town where I saw you pitch? I was up in Illinois for more than a week."

"It was Galesburg," Coley told him.

"Yeah, Galesburg. Galesburg. You had good stuff that day. You were strong out there."

"I had good stuff that day," said Coley. "I didn't know you were there, but my coach told me after the game. My ankle was healed by then."

"I heard about the ankle. What kind of injury was it?"

"It was only a sprain, but it was a bad one."

"Did you have surgery on it?"

Coley didn't want to talk too much about injuries. He knew that injuries were like red flags to scouts. "No, no surgery. The ankle's fine now. Coach told me you used to pitch for the White Sox."

"Six years for the Sox, and a little more than three with the Pirates. I scouted for them for about five years before I took this job with the Royals. So what can I do for you, Coley Burke? What brings you to Fort Myers?"

Even though Coley had given plenty of thought to this moment, now that it was here, he knew that choosing the words would not be easy. Luckily he had a few moments to gather himself while Ricci got up to pour himself another cup of coffee.

"I'd like to throw for you," he said to Ricci, just after the scout resumed his seat.

"Good. I'd love to watch you throw. But why me? Why us?"

"Well, I can tell you this much. I'd like to play for the Royals."

"Great. I'm sure we'd love to have you. But we can't always get what we want. There's a thing called the player draft, and unfortunately the other teams get picks too." Ricci was grinning.

"I know about the major-league draft," said Coley sheepishly. He shifted his weight from one hip to the other. There was a framed eight-by-ten photo on the desk of Bobby Ricci and three famous players—Willie Stargell, Roberto Clemente, and Dale Murphy. They all had golf clubs. The picture was probably taken at one of those celebrity tournaments that raise money for charity.

"In our computer," Ricci continued, "you're already a second-round pick, or third at the latest. Plus, I saw you pitch. You don't have much to prove to us."

Coley sat up straighter. He moistened his lips before he moved the moment to its crisis: "I thought if I could throw for you, you might take me in the first round."

"Mm-hm!"

"I know it's askin' a lot, but I want to be here, in Fort Myers. I want to pitch in the Gulf Coast League."

Ricci shifted suddenly into a mode that was clearly more business-like. "Do you have an agent, son?"

Coley shook his head emphatically. "No, I do not. I've never even talked to an agent. My dad would never let me."

"Does your dad know you're here?"

"No, he doesn't. I'm just here on my own. All I want is to throw for you, and you can decide if I belong in the first round. That's it. That's all of it."

Ricci seemed to lose his edge. He leaned back in his chair and locked both hands behind his neck. "Have you graduated high school?"

Other than the agent question, none of the scout's inquiries was a surprise to Coley. "No, not yet. I'll be graduating a little later on. I'm just down in Florida on a little vacation, sort of."

"Well, we're nearly at the end of May; I guess it's not spring break."

"No, it's not spring break. It's a different kind of vacation. Our school year isn't over till the middle of June."

Ricci sat up straighter and put his elbows on his desk. "Well, I'd love to see you throw. But I'm off to Tampa in about twenty minutes, so it can't be today. How about tomorrow?"

"Tomorrow would be fine. What time?"

"How about this time, say ten thirty? How about ten thirty?"

"Perfect. The only equipment I've got with me is my shoes, though."

"You bring the shoes, we'll take care of anything else you need."

"Great. See you then."

The success of this encounter left him so relieved he was nearly euphoric; but euphoria was not comfortable. He didn't want to go back and deal with Bree right away. He needed to be alone. He drove without a destination, following 41 north across the Caloosahatchee River, east on Pine Island Road, clear through the city of Cape Coral. He ended up on Little Pine Island.

He sat on a beach picnic table for the longest time, confused and disoriented, as though lifted out of time and space. He stared across the water at the Pine Island National Wildlife Refuge, watching the herons and the cranes sail in and out of sight. It was breezy, so the water was rough. He thought about calling his mother again but realized reluctantly that where there were other people, there were agendas. And most of them were over his head. He just wanted to be alone. He soon fell asleep on the sand and didn't awaken until the middle of the afternoon.

He was starving. On his drive back he stopped at a Burger King, where he devoured two Whoppers rapidly and washed them down with a large chocolate shake.

Back at the motel he found Bree down on the beach wearing a brand-new pink thong bikini. It was almost like she was naked. She was searching the water's edge for seashells. She was the most improbable woman-child. Coley scratched his head. Looking up at the terrace by the tiki bar, he saw several of the middle-aged (and older) men staring at her. Her father probably looked like any one of them. It disgusted him to think of any old fart like that mounting Bree. He stared them down until they turned their eyes in different directions.

"How d'you like it?" she asked him. She meant the bikini, of course.

"I think it's absolutely fabulous. I won't be able to control myself. Neither will all those old farts up there by the bar."

"You're not going to be that way. We're in Florida now."

"That's where we are. This would be Florida."

"Well, now that we're here, this is the style."

"There's a difference between the style and the cutting edge, Bree."

"You can say what you want, but I like the suit a lot, and nothing you can say is going to ruin it."

"I'm not trying to ruin anything. I said I like the suit. Where'd you get it?"

"At a mall in Fort Myers Beach."

"How'd you get there?"

"I took the bus."

"You could've waited till I got back. I would've taken you shopping."

"I know, Coley, but I got restless. You were gone so long. I got a Walkman, too. It's in the motel room."

"Terrific." He left abruptly to walk up to the threshold of the terrace. He dragged two of the webbed recliners down to the water's edge. "Sit down," he told her, "so we can talk."

They reclined on the lounges. Each time the tide came in, it scattered foam around the aluminum feet. "I talked to Ricci this morning."

"What'd he say?"

"I get to throw for him tomorrow. At ten thirty."

"Oh, Coley, that's wonderful!"

He sighed. "It's not wonderful. It's good, though."

"But it's wonderful if you can be a pitcher in the Gulf Coast League, isn't it? That's the answer to all our dreams!"

He felt the urge to tell her how little money a player in the Gulf Coast League earned. Instead, he asked her, "Did you call the clinic?"

"They didn't have one in Fort Myers."

"Yeah, okay. What about Cape Coral?"

"Yeah, they have one there. I talked to this woman."

"Okay, so who was 'this woman'?"

"I think she was, like, an appointment person or a receptionist."

"So did you make an appointment?"

Bree was fussing at her hair with hairpins and a pink scrunchie. She didn't look in his direction. "Not exactly," she finally said.

"Not exactly? What's that mean?"

"I'll tell you, but you can't be mad at me."

"I'm not mad, Bree. Tell me."

"But you have to promise you won't be mad, okay?"

Coley could feel himself slump. He wouldn't have had enough energy to be mad. He let his feet fall over the edge of the chaise so they rested in the sand. The surging tide rushed between his toes. "Just tell me."

"They say I have to come in for counseling first."

"So?"

"They say I might have to come in for two sessions."

"So what's wrong with that? Abortion is a surgery. You can't have a surgery without talking to the doctor first."

"But I'll be scared, Coley. You know how I hate it when people ask all the personal questions."

"Bree, they may not ask you personal questions. They'll probably just be giving you information and telling you about your options."

"But I will be scared. What if they ask me about Burns or my real dad? What am I supposed to tell them?"

"You don't have to be scared, I'll go with you. You remember when I sprained my ankle? I had to have consultations, and they didn't even end up doing an operation. The truth is, you'd be more nervous without the counseling."

"Please don't bring up that ankle again."

"It's just an example. Just to make a point."

"Okay," she said, sitting up on the edge of her lounger. "I get the point."

"And you won't even have to go by yourself. I'll go with you. If you want me to, that is."

"I'll have to think it over," she declared. "I have to go change now. You can wait for me here if you want; I'll be back." With that, she left.

Coley watched her from behind for thirty yards or so, until the sun hurt his eyes. Her ass was naked and the only thing across her back was the pink string, which looked about as substantial as a thread.

"I'll have to think it over"? What the hell did that mean? He watched the gulls swooping at the water's edge, fighting over a morsel of fish or one of the tiny, scurrying sand crabs. His gaze wandered out to sea, and he couldn't help but think of the desperate old fisherman in *The Old Man and the Sea*. It almost made him laugh out loud; it seemed so comical that he would choose this time and this place to reflect on books and Mrs. Grissom and English class.

Chapter Sixteen

For supper, they ate stuffed-crab salad at the tiki bar. Afterwards Coley stretched out in the hot tub, which was located near the swimming pool. He had the unit to himself, although there were children and their parents in the pool. There was no pain of any kind in his ankle anymore. Tomorrow, when he threw for Bobby Ricci, there would be no holding back.

Bree came out to sit beside him for a while, but she seemed listless. She was dressed demurely in a Reebok T-shirt and a pair of blue shorts that reached nearly to her knees.

"Hey, Bree, I'm horny. You wanna mess around?"

"Not tonight, Coley. I'm tired."

"Tired from what?"

"I'm not sure. It must be all the stress catching up with me."

"You're thinking about all the questions they might ask you in a counseling session, aren't you?"

"Maybe that's it."

"I told you I'll go with you."

She told him she didn't want to talk about it anymore. She went back to the motel room.

It was nearly midnight when Bree was watching some sci-fi movie on TV and Coley got into the shower. He lathered himself absentmindedly while anticipating how good his stuff would be at Lee County Stadium. If he could show Ricci enough, he might be a first-round pick, but he wasn't one yet. It was pressure, even though his ankle was sound.

He was in the process of toweling himself off when he lifted the lid of the toilet to take a leak. And there it was. Suspended on the surface of the toilet bowl water, it hung motionless like a dead mouse. It still held enough blood to pinken the water. It was a tampon.

It was a tampon. Coley stared at it a minute or two while the reality it represented was sinking in. It was *Bree's* tampon. She wasn't pregnant. He took a deep breath. *Oh, wonderful,* he thought to himself. *This is just perfect.*

When he was finished drying off, he wrapped the towel tightly around his waist. Gingerly he fished the tampon out of the toilet bowl by its string tail and held it up between thumb and forefinger in a pincer grip. He watched dumbly while the drops tumbled down to land in the toilet, splashing their pale pink hue the instant they contacted the water's surface.

He wasn't sure what he intended to do with the dead soldier, but when it was dry enough that drops fell only every five seconds or so, he held it at about shoulder level and leaned against the door frame. Bree was propped up against the headboard of the bed, still watching her movie.

"Hey, Bree. Look what I found."

She looked in his direction before she used the mute button on the remote to turn off the sound. "What did you say?"

The tampon was swinging from its string like a visual aid a hypnotist might use. "Look what I found."

"What is it?" But she was turning white even as she asked the question.

"It's either a dead mouse or a tampon. I haven't figured it out yet."

"What would you be doing with a tampon?" she asked.

"That's a good question. But here's a better one: What would *you* be doing with a tampon?"

"I don't know what you're talking about. I'm sure I don't know where that tampon came from."

"I suppose it came from somebody else's room. Maybe room 122 or one up on the second floor. Room 200, for instance."

"Why are you being so sarcastic? What are you saying to me?"

"I'm sayin' you're not pregnant, Bree. You flushed the tampon down, but it didn't stay down. It came back up."

The tears in her eyes came quickly. "Now you'll be mad at me, won't you?"

But it all seemed so absurd, Coley was surprised to find how little anger he did feel. "You're not pregnant. You lied."

"I didn't lie about that, I really thought I was pregnant."

"Why did you think so? Because of that stupid home pregnancy test you told me about?"

"No, not that, the test was inconclusive."

"Inconclusive?"

"I wasn't exactly sure how to read the results. You have to believe me."

He sat on the edge of the bed and took a deep breath. If this whole thing weren't so desperate, it might be comical. "Okay, it wasn't the test. What made you think you were pregnant?"

The tears were rolling down her cheeks. "I was more than a month late. I thought I was pregnant."

"I told you bein' late a few weeks might not mean anything. Anybody could have told you the same thing."

"But I thought I was, I really did."

"You're havin' your period right now. That's why you're not in the mood for sex. That's why you had to get out of your swimsuit so fast. Look me right in the eye and tell me I'm wrong."

She didn't look up when she said, "But I didn't lie to you, Coley, truly I didn't. I thought I was pregnant. Please don't be mad at me."

It was odd how he felt sorry for her. When men were mad at her, they beat her up or they used her for gratification. He felt sorry for her, but not mad. "I'm not mad at you, Bree. I'm just disgusted with myself."

She was using the back of her hand to wipe her tears. "This doesn't have to change things, Coley. We're still in love and we're still on our own. You can pitch and we can still make it."

He wasn't listening, though. He was headed out the door, seeking the darkness of the terrace where it joined the beach. "Just don't follow me. I need to be by myself."

He didn't care at all about pitching for Bobby Ricci or any of the other Royals player personnel. But he did it anyway. He figured he'd made the appointment so he had to honor it. Besides which, it would get him away from Bree for most of the day.

It was probably due to the fact that he didn't give a damn that his performance was so superb. No pressure. He found himself plunged into a thoughtless state of being where nothing could intrude.

Ricci gave him a pair of generic baseball pants to wear, a Royals cap and a three-quarter-sleeve undershirt. He got loose along the third-base line, throwing to an ex-big-league catcher named Eby Rosen.

Then Ricci wanted him to pitch from the mound. There were two other men standing near home plate too, but Coley didn't know their names. They both had speed guns. Either he didn't get their names, or he didn't care to remember.

Maybe this was what it had always been like for Patrick. You brought all the heat, all the time, with an utter disregard for the rest of the world. Maybe that was the killer instinct: disregard.

Coley's fastball was blazing and tailing sharply. His slider had a nasty bite. Everything he threw was around the plate and alive. Then he pitched to a right-handed batter named Gary Hoyle, who was from some area junior college. Coley didn't know if he was a prospect or not, and he didn't care. Under other conditions he might have been nervous. But not on this day. He just kept striking him out. Hoyle couldn't catch up with the high heat, and when Coley threw him a couple of cut fastballs, they were in on his hands so tight they practically sawed his bat off.

Gary Hoyle might just as well have been the Reggie Jackson statue in the backyard, except he was right-handed. Coley visualized the statue in his mind's eye and hated it. He hated all it was and all it stood for. He unleashed a 95 mph fastball under Gary Hoyle's chin.

When Ricci told him to stop, Coley was sweating profusely but he wasn't tired. He felt like he could keep on going forever. He only wished there were no other time and no other place and no other people in the whole world.

When he took a seat behind home plate, though, his high energy level vanished almost immediately. He hadn't had much sleep the night before, not after the confrontation with Bree over the pregnancy scam, and he hadn't eaten any breakfast this morning on his way to the stadium. The sweat rolled down his face while Ricci gave him compliments.

"We had you at ninety-four on the speed gun at least a dozen times," the scout told him.

Ninety-four, Coley thought. He couldn't remember ever throwing that hard consistently.

"Even better," Ricci continued, "your ball is live. It's got that nice tail and a downward motion. Your slider is better than it oughta be in a pitcher your age."

"So what are you saying to me?"

"I'm saying you're a helluva pitcher with a helluva future."

"Thanks," Coley replied. But he wondered glumly what the future might be, with Bree back at the motel room, not pregnant at all, and the two of them on the run. "You think maybe you'll want me in the first round?"

"Maybe," said Ricci. "Can't promise anything. We might need a shortstop more. You might not be available when it's our pick. That's the way it is anytime you have a player draft, everything is maybe."

"I want to pitch in the Gulf Coast League," was all Coley could think to say.

"Yeah, you told me." Ricci had a cigar out. He was using his tongue to moisten at least two inches of it. Coley wondered why people did that when they smoked cigars. "There's something else I think," said Ricci.

"What's that?"

"It's none of my business, really, but I think maybe you've got something goin' on. Something you need to take care of."

"Oh, really." Coley didn't look in Bobby Ricci's face. Instead, he used an available towel to wipe the sweat from his face and neck.

"I don't know what it is, and I'm not gonna ask. But you wanna make sure you get your mind right."

"I haven't told you any lies about bein' down here," said Coley. He didn't take the time to add that most of his truths had been essentially half-truths.

"I didn't say anything about lying, and you don't need to tell me anything. But a great arm will only take you so far unless you've got your mind right. That's all I'm gonna say."

"I better go," said Coley. He stood up to shake Ricci's hand. "You'll keep in touch, right?"

By the time he made his way back to the motel, it was past 7 P.M. He had a couple of McDonald's Quarter Pounders in a carryout sack and two large Cokes. Bree was glad; she said she was starving.

They ate this supper while sitting on beach chairs from the terrace down at the water's edge. "Where have you been all this time?" she asked him.

"I was pitching for Bobby Ricci."

"How'd it go?"

"I was awesome," he replied in a flat voice. "I was Sandy Koufax."

"That's wonderful, Coley. But who is Sandy Koufax?"

"He's just an old pitcher from a long time ago. He's in the Hall of Fame."

"You'll be in the Hall of Fame too, I know you will. But where were you the rest of the time?"

"I was at the airport. I was drinkin' beer and watchin' the planes fly in and out."

"How did you get the beer?"

Coley had his mouth full of hamburger, so he couldn't answer right away. He swallowed, and drank some of the Coke. "I can't say for sure, they just didn't card me."

"I can't understand why you'd want to sit in the airport so long. You could've been back here with me, swimming or scuba diving or anything. It's because you're still mad at me, aren't you?"

He ignored the question. "I was timin' the planes, Bree. With my watch. Sometimes they come in two minutes apart, sometimes four minutes. One time it was almost ten minutes."

"Boring, boring. The truth is, you're still mad at me." Her sandwich finished, she took hold of his hand. "You still think I was lying, but I wasn't really. I cleaned up our room today, by the way."

"You cleaned up our room? You cleaned up our motel room?"

"Yes, I did."

"They have *maids* for that. Nobody cleans up a motel room."

"But the maids don't do the laundry and fold up the clothes in the dresser drawers. Those are the things I did."

This was no subject to pursue. He removed his hand so as to pick up his cup. "The truth is, I'm mad at myself. I've been doin' all my thinking with my dick. Ever since I met you, Bree, that's what I've been doing. We both know it."

"You can't say that, Coley. It makes it sound like I don't love you."

"It's supposed to sound like this: You tell me I'm smart, but you're the one who's smart. At least you think with your head."

"I can't tell what that's supposed to mean."

"Think about it, maybe it'll come to you."

Then they were both silent for several minutes. The wind was up, so the gulls were in a higher pattern to take advantage of the force. A stronger tide pounded in with each surge. Coley finally said, "This is where Patrick died."

"Your brother died right here?"

"Not here exactly. It was farther up the coast, near Tampa, at a place called Longboat Key. That's when the Mets were still training at Tampa."

"Do you really want to talk about something so sad?"

"He was in a speedboat with two other guys. They were all drunk out of their mind. They crashed their boat into a pier, but

Patrick was the only one killed. The other two were in the hospital for about six months."

Bree took his arm with both her hands but didn't speak.

"Patrick was stupid," Coley continued in a hollow voice. "He was one dumb son of a bitch. He could have been a great pitcher. He could have been a star."

"Don't say he was stupid, though. That seems too disrespectful."

"He was a stupid son of a bitch because he wasted all his talent. He spent his life livin' on the edge, so it was bound to happen. And all for what? For absolutely nothin'. My mother was always right about him."

"Maybe you shouldn't talk about this anymore."

He ignored her. "And that's why I feel so sorry for her. Because she was always right, but he's still dead."

She gripped his arm tighter. "Coley, why are you telling me all of this? I don't like the way you're talking."

He turned to look at her. "When I was at the airport, I did something else, Bree. I bought airline tickets."

"You did what?"

"I said I bought plane tickets. We're going back home. Tomorrow you and I are out of here."

"Oh! You can't be serious." She released his arm dramatically. It was astonishing how swiftly her green eyes made their transformation from deep to flat. She flopped back on her recliner.

"I'm very serious. Our flight leaves at nine fifteen in the morning."

"You're just doing this to punish me. You think I lied to you, and this is how you want me to pay for it."

"I don't want you to pay for anything, Bree. It's time to go back."

"How can you even think of doing this to me? Can you imagine what Burns will do to me?"

Coley nodded his head before he answered, "I've thought of it." He was surprised at his own inner calm and had to wonder if it stemmed from finally doing *the right thing*.

"Have you thought how he'll beat me?"

"I told you I've thought of it. I don't think he'll beat you."

"How can you be so stupid? Of course he will. What have I been telling you all this time? D'you think you can beat him up or something?"

"I don't know if I can or not."

"Then what are you saying?" At least she was looking at him again.

"I'm not going to fight him. Even if I could beat him up, I'm not going to fight him. I'm going to give him an offer he can't refuse."

"Oh, really. D'you think this is like the *movies* or something? This is reality."

"No, I don't think it's the movies. I just think he'll listen to reason."

"I can't believe what you're saying to me. You just decide all by yourself that we're going back, so you go to the airport and buy tickets. What about me? What about what *I* want?"

"I'm not forgetting about you, Bree, believe me."

"Why should I believe you? You act like this whole thing is just about *you*."

"For once I agree with you. This whole thing *is* about me. It never has been, not since I met you. I haven't made a single decision, at least not a real one. This is a real one, and it's all mine."

"I have no idea what you're talking about."

"You will, though. Sooner or later, you will."

Chapter Seventeen

On the return flight she gave him the silent treatment. For the moment, he felt compelled to try to explain to her how he perceived their relationship. "To tell you the truth, Bree, I don't think you know any more about being in love than I do."

But her only response was to put a tape in her new Walkman and fit the headphones over her ears. Coley didn't mind. Maybe it was better this way, maybe she wouldn't be interrupting him to ask if he was mad or to beg him to forgive her for lying. Maybe he would say it better this way. "The point is," he told her, "none of this was ever an accident. None of it just happened."

She wasn't listening, of course. She had cranked up the only tape she had with her, *Butterfly,* by Maria Carey. The volume was up loud enough that Coley could hear traces of it himself. The music was slipping out from beneath the edges of the foam pads that covered her ears. He went on: "You knew I had just broken up with Gloria, and you thought I was cool. Everybody thinks I'm cool. I get written up in the sports pages, I get interviewed on TV, and blah, blah. I'm supposed to be a major-league pitcher someday. Plus I'm supposed to get rich."

The flight attendant came by with a cart. She offered them a Coke or a Sprite, but only Coley took one.

He took a sip before he continued, "You figured if you got pregnant, or at least if we *thought* you were pregnant, we would get married. Then live happily ever after, I guess. Me as a big-league star, you with lots of money to spend, the two of us layin' out on the beaches of Cancun or the Bahamas. But think about how lame it all was, really.

"Who knows what might have been if that tampon had flushed away the way you thought it would? Not me. I can't blame you for the things you do, though, not after the way you've been treated by Burns and your real dad. That's why I'm not mad at you. The truth is, I feel sorry for you, which is probably worse than being mad. I love the sex we have and I pity you. That doesn't make for much of a relationship, not a real one anyway."

He stopped talking so he could finish his Coke. Bree's head had fallen to the side. Was she asleep? "You've had lots of problems, Bree, but you'll never get out from under 'em by running away. The way Bobby Ricci puts it, we have to get our minds right. We can't do that by running away."

When they landed at O'Hare, they found the car right where they'd left it, in the long-term parking section. It hadn't been towed, it wasn't chained down, it didn't even have a ticket or note on the windshield. Paying the bill reminded Coley they'd been gone only four days. It felt more like four weeks.

The drive home took the same length of time—three and a half hours—as the flight had. But it was more of an endurance test for Coley. Bree was as sullen and silent as she'd been on the plane, and he felt thoroughly exhausted from the sleepless nights and the emotional trauma that had drained him throughout this Florida fiasco.

Once, during the drive, when he asked her if she was hungry, she ignored his question altogether. But she did remove her headphones long enough to remind him, "He's going to beat me, you know."

"Not that again, okay? I told you I'm going to deal with that."

"I don't know how you think you are. Then after he beats me, he'll probably hit my mother because she'll try to protect me."

Her remarks opened up his nerves despite his guarded optimism. What lay ahead for both of them could be ugly. The consequences were too much to think about. "Can you trust me on this?" he finally asked.

"I don't know why I should. You're still thinking of yourself." Without waiting for any response, she slipped the headphones back into place.

Coley didn't get really nervous until he pulled the car around the corner at the end of her block. It was late afternoon.

He was lifting her suitcases out of the trunk when Burns came out the door and across the lawn, walking so rapidly he was nearly jogging. He might have been running but for the beach thongs that flopped on his feet. He was wearing a Hawaiian shirt and a pair of blue shorts.

The confrontation, the part where he got right up in Coley's face, nose-to-nose almost, occurred halfway up the sidewalk. Coley put the suitcases down. He spread his feet just slightly, for balance. If there was going to be a fight, he was ready. "Back off," he said to the stepfather.

"Who the hell do you think you are?"

"I said back off. Get out of my space." Suddenly his nerves were not the nerves of fear and apprehension, but those of a swift and sure adrenaline rush. Like getting ready to strike out a batter in a clutch situation.

"And I said, who the hell do you think you are? You're probably on your way to jail, you know that?"

"Stop it," Bree demanded. "Both of you have to just stop it."

From the corner of his eye Coley could see her mother hurrying out the front door.

"I wouldn't know where to start with you," said Burns. "What

I'd like to do is just knock the shit out of you right here and now."

"You can try," said Coley. "Bree says that's your usual method."

This remark seemed to catch him up short, if only briefly. He hesitated slightly before he said, "Do you think because you're a big sports star you can do anything you want? You think laws are for other people?" The big man kept opening and closing his fingers. Fists, then no fists. Then fists again.

"No, I don't think that," Coley told him. "What I'd like to do is apologize, but if you don't back off of me, I'm just gonna leave."

"Let him apologize," said Bree's mother. She had the helpless look on her face Coley associated with news film of forlorn mothers in refugee camps.

Burns didn't take his eyes from Coley's, but he did step back, a full pace. "So you think an apology can make up for what you've done?"

"No, I don't think it can. What we did was wrong, and it was mostly my fault, not Bree's. I'm sorry. For what it's worth, I'm sorry."

"Bree's not even sixteen yet. You can go to jail for kidnapping, aggravated sexual assault, probably even rape. Have you thought at all about the consequences for what you've done?"

"Yes and no," Coley answered. "Not enough, that's for sure." At least there wasn't going to be a fight. The two of them were still squared off, alert and balanced, with Bree and her mother clinging somewhere in between, trying to act as buffers and stay out of the way at the same time.

"Apologies aren't going to cut it, Coley Burke. What you've done goes beyond that, way beyond. As soon as we press charges, you'll be facing an arrest warrant, and if you're lucky, it'll be only one."

Coley felt calmer now. All of this was going more or less the way he'd expected. He said, "You'll do what you have to do, I guess. But I want to give you somethin' to think about."

"What would that be?"

"Our family lawyer is Stanley Irlbacher. You've probably heard of him; he's the best attorney in town."

"You can't throw that country club shit at me," said Burns with contempt. "I move in those same circles myself."

"Okay, then, let me throw this shit at you." He pointed at Bree and said, "I know that you hit her. Sometimes you slap her and sometimes you hit her with your fist. She's told me all about it. I've seen the cuts and I've seen the bruises. Maybe you'd like to deal with that in open court."

"You don't stand here on my lawn and make accusations. What goes on in this family is our business, and you're out of bounds to make presumptions." But Coley had seen him flinch. No more fists, either.

"Any chickenshit that likes to slap around women and girls makes it everybody's business. There's no privacy that goes with that. I'm no genius, but even I know that."

"Are you threatening me? Are you standing in front of my family and threatening me?"

"I'm tellin' you this: I don't have a lot of friends on the high school staff, but I do have one. Her name is Mrs. Alvarez, and she's a counselor. If you ever lay a hand on Bree again, I'll know about it. One way or another, I'll know about it."

"You're threatening me with a high school counselor?"

"You could say that. Because as soon as I know it, Mrs. Alvarez will know about it. Here's how the law works: If a school counselor has even a *suspicion* that a student is being abused, they have to report it to the authorities." He thought about adding that this point of law was something he'd learned in human dynamics class but figured that would sound too juvenile.

"You are threatening me."

"Call it what you want. But the way it would go would be like this. Mrs. Alvarez tells DCFS, they tell the cops, and then it goes to the district attorney's office. You can figure out the rest. It would be sort of like a chain of command. You would know all about that from your years in the military."

"Okay, you've made your point, now drop it."

But he wasn't ready to drop it, not quite yet. He said, "The difference is that this is not the military. Bree and your wife aren't under your command. Besides, even in the army I doubt if they let the officers slap the troops around. You tell me."

"I said you've made your point. We're not going to resolve all of this here and now." Burns put his hands on his hips. He went into a lot of neck stretching and shoulder flexing, but what was clear was that he was looking for a way to save face. It was damage control time. He turned to Bree. "Are you okay, baby?"

"I'm okay."

"Did he hurt you?"

There were tears running down her cheeks as she looked in Coley's direction. "I'm okay. He didn't do anything to hurt me. Coley never hurts me."

Burns put his arm around her shoulder before he turned his face back to Coley. "I'd say emotions are running a little high at this point," he suggested. His voice was much more subdued, to go right along with his body language. "Maybe we'd all be better off if we declared a sort of cooling-off period."

Even Bree's mother seemed a little relieved at this point. "You need to go home, Coley. Your parents have been worried terribly. Your poor mother and I have been on the phone half a dozen times."

"Yeah, I know. I'm ashamed about it." He knew it was time to go home. But before he turned to leave, he said to Bree, "I'll see you soon, Bree. I'm not sure just what the circumstances are gonna be like, but I'll see you soon. And I'm sorry, I really am."

"Go home now, Coley," said her mother. "Your mother needs to see you."

"I'm on my way." To Burns he issued one last reminder. "Just remember what I said."

Chapter Eighteen

On the fifth of June, Coley sat on the hood of his car beyond the outfield fence, watching the play-offs. If the team won today, it would mean a regional championship, which would put them in the sectionals. It didn't look likely, though; they were already behind. Quintero was pitching. He would be good someday, but he wasn't ready yet.

Sitting in this remote location allowed him to satisfy his curiosity, but without having to worry about causing any distraction. It was enormously painful. He wanted to be here, but he couldn't be part of it. He glanced up at the sky, where the gathering clouds indicated rain was on the way. Why not? It seemed like it had rained every day all week.

That was when Ruthie Roth showed up. Coley hadn't noticed her approach, but she was suddenly next to him, leaning against the fender. "Is this seat taken?" she asked him.

He smiled before he answered. "These are just the general admission seats. Like bleacher seats. First come, first served. Are you a baseball fan now, Ruthie?"

"I think you know better than that. I've been up in the newspaper office. They asked me to write an article about National Honor Society for the last issue of the year."

"So did you write it?"

"I was going to, but then I changed my mind. Instead I decided to write an article called 'Coley and Bree's Excellent Adventure.'" She was smiling.

Coley's grin was sheepish. He looked down. "So you heard about that."

"Heard about it? I may be out of the loop, Coley, but I'm not off the planet. Everybody in school heard about it. You two are lucky it wasn't in the papers."

"Yeah, we were lucky. That would be the word." He turned his attention back to the game, where Rico was batting. On the third pitch he got a line-drive single to left. "Yes!" Coley declared in a high-decibel whisper. He pumped his fist.

"God, this must be hard on you," said Ruthie.

He looked at her. It seemed like the softest thing she'd ever said to him. It sounded *sympathetic*. He decided to take the risk. "Hard on me? Only like I've got a knife stuck in my gut, which gets twisted every once in a while."

"I know you talked to Mrs. Alvarez. What'd she tell you?"

He sighed. "I'm suspended for the rest of the term, but I can make up my work. If I pass English in summer school, I can graduate."

"So you can go to Bradley after all."

"If I pass with at least a C."

"You can do it, don't worry. If you're in summer school, you'll probably have Miss Titus. You'll like her."

"Well, at least it won't be Grissom anymore."

"What about professional baseball, Coley? What about the major leagues?"

"If I get drafted in the first round, I'll probably sign."

"And what if you don't? Not that I have a clue what being drafted is."

"If you get drafted in the first round, it means you get a big-money contract."

"You don't seem very excited about it."

He watched Kershaw strike out to end the inning. "I'm not," he told her. "I'm too ashamed right now to get wired up about much of anything. I have to graduate high school. I need to get my mind right. If I don't go first round, I'll spend a year at Bradley. After that, I can reenter the draft if I want to."

"I can't follow all of this," Ruthie admitted. "What about Bree?"

"The same thing. She's suspended, but she can make up her work."

"Are you still seeing her?"

"I don't actually see her. We talk on the phone once in a while." Coley asked her, "Why are you bein' so nice to me?"

"You don't kick people when they're down, right?"

"Right." It made sense. "Long as you're here, Ruthie, how'd you like to do me a favor?"

"That would depend on the favor."

"Did you ever drive a tractor?"

"Did I ever drive a tractor? I'd say about as often as I've climbed Mount Everest."

"In other words, you haven't. I could teach you easy, though, and you could do me a favor."

"You still haven't told me what it is you're asking me to do."

"Get in the car. I want you to help me move a statue. All you'll have to do is drive a lawn tractor. Afterwards I'll take you home."

"What about the game?"

"I'm curious, but like I told you, it hurts to watch. I'm ready to go now."

"What if I refuse to do this favor?"

"I'll still take you home. Get in. Please?"

When they got to Coley's house, no one was home. He was grateful but not surprised; after all, it was just after four.

Coley pulled the lawn tractor out onto the driveway and let it run in neutral.

"Is this what you expect me to drive?" Ruthie asked him.

"There's nothin' to it, really. It's got hydrostatic drive."

"What does that mean?"

"It means you don't have to worry about usin' a clutch. It's like a car with automatic transmission. Come on." He drove the tractor around back so he could position it next to the statue.

Ruthie Roth had never been to Coley's home before. She was deeply impressed by the beauty of the landscaping. "Who does all of this?"

"My mom, mostly. She gets a little help from Trinh sometimes. He's the yardman."

There was a chain in the utility box that Coley used to secure a tight loop around Reggie Jackson's waist, where the indentations from all the fastballs that had plunked it were numerous. Then he secured the other end to the back of the tractor, leaving about twelve feet of slack.

"I won't even ask what this statue is all about," said Ruthie. "It's bizarre, though."

"My mother would agree with you," he laughed.

"But I have to ask what we're doing here, and how much trouble can I get myself into?"

"No trouble at all. My parents won't even know who did it. They'll just think I did it by myself."

"So why don't you do it by yourself then?"

"Because there are too many tight spots. Somebody has to walk behind to keep the statue on course. Otherwise it'll be knocking down flowers and bushes and God knows what else. Besides, we have to pull it through that narrow space between the garage and the fence."

"And then what?"

"We're gonna drag the son of a bitch up the road to the bridge. We're gonna throw it into Laurel Creek and watch it float away. It can float clear to the ocean, for all I care."

Ruthie was already shaking her head before he'd finished his sentence. "There's no ocean anywhere near Laurel Creek, which I'm sure you already know. But what makes you think it's going to float?"

"Because the water's so high from all the rain we've had. The creek has a real swift current now."

She was shaking her head again. She knocked on the torso of the statue with her knuckles. "This thing is hollow, right?"

"It's hollow, but it's heavy as hell."

"Coley, it's not going to float depending on the swiftness of the current. The only thing that will determine if it floats or not is how much water it displaces."

"What's that supposed to mean?" He felt a raindrop, and then another. He got onto the seat and surged the tractor forward twice. He could hear a cracking sound at the base of the statue, where the footings were bolted down. On the third try the statue came tumbling down, making a dull *thud* in the grass. Coley went back to take a look. The concrete base was broken into pieces where the rusted bolts were sheared off. There was a huge divot near Reggie's right elbow that would have embarrassed any golfer.

"This is about the weirdest thing I've ever seen," Ruthie declared. "You've got this huge metal statue of some baseball player—"

"Reggie Jackson."

"Reggie Jackson, then, whoever that is. It's probably worth a lot of money, although it would go against any logic. You just pulled it down and now you want to throw it in the creek."

He felt a few more raindrops. "Okay, it's weird. That's something we agree on. What were you sayin' about how it's goin' to float?"

"I was saying, that will depend on water displacement. It will float if the amount of liquid that is displaced is the same or less than the hull. That's Archimedes' principle."

"Oh."

"Simple physics."

"In my mind there's no such thing as simple physics. I was lucky to get through Basic Math II. Now get on up here in the seat. Please. It's gonna rain soon."

She did as he requested but asked him, "Why am I doing this?"

"Because I asked you to. Because we're friends."

"Friends," said Ruthie, repeating the word thoughtfully. Coley knew now that she was going to drive the tractor, but he could tell at the same time it wouldn't be right away. It must have been something about the word *friends* that got stuck somewhere, because she had her glasses off. She was using a handkerchief to clean them. It was hard for Coley to determine if she was simply wiping off raindrops or working toward some kind of composure.

When she had her glasses on again, she said to him, "I'm ready, I guess. Show me."

Ruthie had no problem steering the tractor, partly because she insisted on driving at the slowest possible speed. That was fine with Coley, though, because it made his job easier. With his right foot he kept shoving the base of the statue into position so it was dragged straight behind the tractor. Using this method, they avoided any damage to flower beds or landscaping stones or the side of the garage.

By the time they made it to the street, the raindrops were more frequent, but Ruthie declared she was enjoying the ride. He

JAMES W. BENNETT

couldn't help smiling. He told her to drive on up the street to the bridge, which was some fifty yards up a gentle incline. She even throttled up. The statue bounced and clunked behind, sparking the blacktop from time to time. Coley walked behind. *I'm gonna plunk you like never before.*

The bridge railing was an old-fashioned one, made of concrete, but it wasn't much more than three feet high. Once they got the statue into the upright position, the hard part would be lifting it onto the railing.

"Once we get it up here," Coley told Ruthie, "we can lay it on its side. The rest will be easy. All we have to do is just push it on over."

They lifted together, on either side of the base. Coley sucked it up and strained his muscles to the utmost. He could tell he was doing most of the lifting by far, but the little bit of help Ruthie provided was just enough to make the difference. The statue was on its side, teetering on the flat surface of the railing. Coley was out of breath; he had to pause several seconds to recover. His pulse was racing. Ruthie was in the same condition, only worse.

Then it was time. The final push was easy. The statue tumbled over and smacked the water with a huge splash. It submerged briefly beneath the water's surface, then ever so slowly, or so it seemed, rose to the top. It floated. It was in motion, carried by the swift current. The two of them stood in the rain, watching it bob its way into the distance until it was hardly more than a speck.

"It floats," said Coley.

"That's displacement for you."

"How far do you think it'll go?" he asked her.

She was cleaning her glasses again, and returning to her old sarcastic self. She said, "Oh, I suppose it'll probably go clear to the ocean."

"Yeah, but which one? The Atlantic or the Pacific?"

"Maybe neither one. Maybe it'll end up down in the Gulf of Mexico."

He hadn't thought of that option. "That would be just about perfect," he said. Then he asked her, "Did I thank you yet?"

"Not that I remember, but that would take social skills."

"Thanks a lot, Ruthie. Come on, I'll take you home."